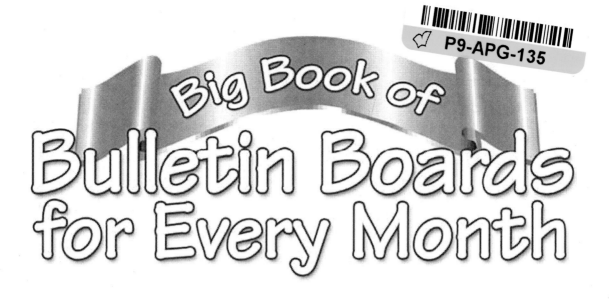

Big Book of Bulletin Boards for Every Month

Jeanne Cheyney
Arnold Cheyney

GOOD YEAR BOOKS

Dedication

To Teachers of Children Everywhere

Good Year Books
Our titles are available for most basic curriculum subjects plus many enrichment areas.
For information on other Good Year Books and to place orders, contact your local
bookseller or educational dealer, or visit our website at www.goodyearbooks.com.
For a complete catalog, please contact:

Good Year Books
10200 Jefferson Boulevard
Culver City, CA 90232-0802
www.goodyearbooks.com

Cover Design: DesignPro Graphics
Text Design: DesignPro Graphics
Drawings: Jeanne Cheyney
Additional Illustrations: Mike Dammer, Wilkinson Studios. Inc.

ISBN-13: 978-1-59647-062-0

 GOOD YEAR BOOKS

PREFACE

Big Book of Bulletin Boards For Every Month includes suggestions for bulletin boards plus patterns. Here are a few general tips to create your own bulletin boards:

1. Cover bulletin boards with solid-colored cloth and add contrasting borders.

2. Extend figures beyond the bulletin board, if you wish; no limits.

3. Use blank walls for larger displays.

4. Scotch Magic™ tape, rolled around a finger, adheres well to walls.

5. Color figures heavily to avoid a washed-out look.

6. Be creative with the patterns and make your own displays.

7. Change them often and let the children help.

8. Enjoy!

LARGE LETTERS

A B C D
E F G H I
J K L M

MATERIALS AND SUPPLIES

- any paper—e.g., construction paper, typing paper, wrapping paper, wallpaper, newspaper (or painted newspaper), grocery bags, table paper, shelf paper
- scissors

iv

NOPQ
RSTU
VWXY
Z

SMALL LETTERS

A B C D E
F G H I J K
L M N O P
Q R S T U
V W X Y Z

MATERIALS AND SUPPLIES
- any paper—e.g., construction paper, typing paper, wrapping paper, wallpaper, newspaper (or painted newspaper), grocery bags, table paper, shelf paper
- scissors

BORDERS

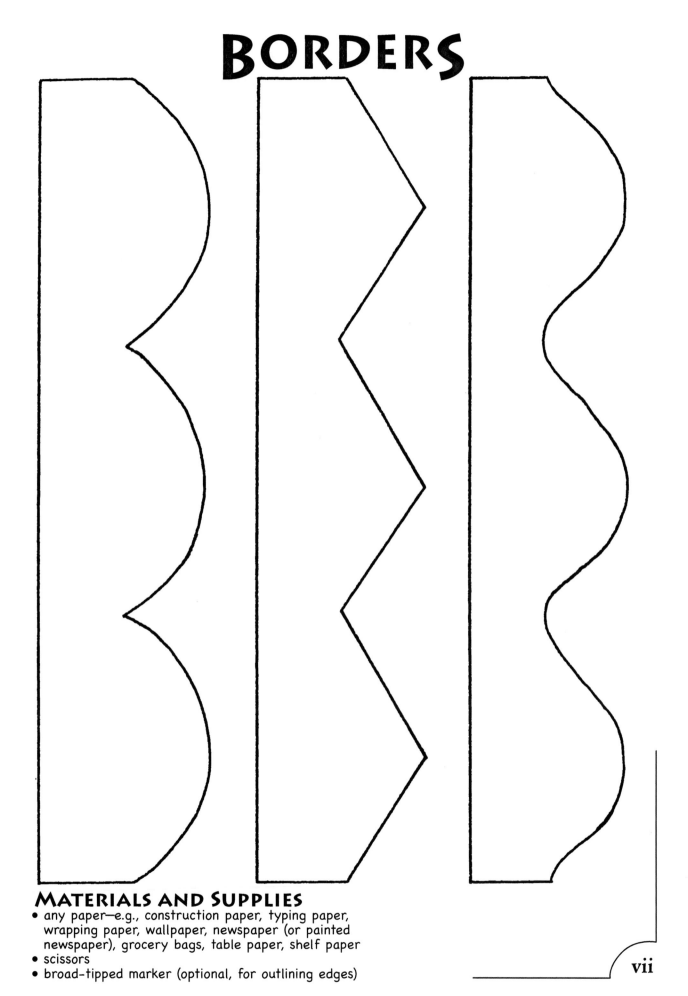

MATERIALS AND SUPPLIES
- any paper—e.g., construction paper, typing paper, wrapping paper, wallpaper, newspaper (or painted newspaper), grocery bags, table paper, shelf paper
- scissors
- broad-tipped marker (optional, for outlining edges)

CONTENTS

November

December

January

February

March

April

May

June

July

August

Project Patterns

Project Patterns (continued)

Project Patterns (continued)

Project Patterns (continued)

SEPTEMBER

MATERIALS AND SUPPLIES

- dark green cloth background
- white border
- white letters

- wide, clear shipping tape
- crayons
- scissors
- glue

- any white paper that crayons can write on (Used computer paper, clean on one side, is OK.)

INSTRUCTIONS

1. Prepare the bulletin board for the first day of school, if desired.

2. Use the boy or girl patterns on pages 103 and 104. (Follow solid lines for boy's hair and dotted lines for girl's hair.) Glue the body parts together at the dotted lines. Color the girl's shirt yellow with a red flower (page 158, pattern A) and her shorts red with yellow flowers. In-line skates are red. Her hair is bright orange. The boy's hair is black and his cap bright blue and white. The shirt is bright blue, the shorts bright orange, and the in-line skates bright blue. Use heavy color.

3. Pencils, page 125, and crayons, page 136, are bright blue, green, and red.

4. Use any bright-colored paper for the two books. Fold papers in half widthwise.

5. Using the pattern on page 154 (pattern A), cut outlines of in-line skates for children's name tags for the first days of school.

6. Let each child draw a skating figure to look like himself or herself. Tape these to the walls around the room.

SEPTEMBER

MATERIALS AND SUPPLIES

- dark green cloth background
- orange border
- orange letters

- any white paper that crayons can write on
- 3 or 4 sheets of lined primary paper

- 3/4" transparent tape
- crayons
- scissors

INSTRUCTIONS

This bulletin board can be used to welcome the children to your class on the first day of school.

1. Using patterns on pages 96 to 101, make and color as many figures as desired. Use your choice of paper for skin colors. Use heavy colors for clothes and facial features.

2. Cut two faces only for top and side of bulletin board and cut three hands from the patterns on page 96. Tape them to the wall.

3. Make crayons and pencils from the patterns on pages 136 and 125. Color heavily. Add sheets of lined primary paper.

SEPTEMBER

MATERIALS AND SUPPLIES

- dark blue cloth background
- white border
- white letters

- wide-tipped black marker
- crayons
- scissors

- any white paper that crayons can write on (Used computer paper, clean on one side, is OK.)

INSTRUCTIONS

1. Discuss any manners that need attention:
   Do I clean up classroom materials?
   Do I answer others nicely?
   Do I say, "Fine, thank you," if someone asks me how I am?
   Do I quietly wait for my turn?
   Do I put playthings away?
   Do I talk with my mouth full of food?
   Do I treat others, including my family, as I want them to treat me?
   If a friend gives me a cookie, do I say, "Thank you"?
   Do I say "Please" if I want something?
   Do I say "Excuse me" if I bump someone?
   If I cough or sneeze, do I cover my mouth or nose with my hand or tissue?

2. Encourage the children, two at a time, to act out these situations and show appropriate responses.

3. Using patterns on pages 105–107, color and cut out faces.

4. On scrap computer paper, cut rectangles 8 ½" by 5½". Using the marker, print these sentences:
   I clean up classroom materials.
   I eat with my mouth closed.
   I put playthings away.
   I say "Excuse me."
   I say "Please."
   I say "Thank you."

5. Let the children draw and color pictures of the good manners listed in #4.

6. Follow up this activity by encouraging children to say "please," "thank you," and "excuse me."

SEPTEMBER

MY FAMILY

MATERIALS AND SUPPLIES

- light green cloth background
- dark green border and letters
- manila or white paper
- crayons
- scissors
- lined paper (optional)
- broad-tipped black and green markers
- cloth or wallpaper (optional)

INSTRUCTIONS

1. Have the children draw pictures of their families and write about them. On the bulletin board, write names only.

2. Prepare the figures from the patterns on pages 110 and 116–117. Color heavily or dress as paper dolls with cloth or wallpaper (optional). Outline in black marker.

3. Add lined or white papers. Outline in green marker.

SEPTEMBER

RED IS . . .

MATERIALS AND SUPPLIES

- bright yellow cloth background
- black border
- black letters
- red, black, and white paper

- broad-tipped black marker
- transparent tape
- crayons
- scissors
- glue

- any white paper that crayons can write on (Used computer paper, clean on one side, is OK.)

INSTRUCTIONS

1. Discuss the color red or any color of your choice.

2. Ask the children to cut something of that color from magazines or newspapers for the bulletin board. (Can labels or bits of yarn or ribbon are possibilities too.)

3. Cut a front view of a red Danny Dibby and parts from the patterns on page 108. Cut black-and-white caps from the pattern on page 109, or color black parts with crayons. Glue arms, legs, and caps in place.

4. If needed, outline Danny and parts with black marker.

5. Make Danny's eyes, nose, and mouth from black or white paper, whichever shows up better. You can use black marker too.

6. Cut four red hands from the arm and hand pattern on page 108.

7. Place Danny Dibby parts around the bulletin board.

5

SEPTEMBER

MATERIALS AND SUPPLIES

- black background
- yellow border and letters
- manila, brown, and white paper
- crayons
- scissors

INSTRUCTIONS

1. Talk about how each class member is unique and how each has his or her good qualities. Emphasize the need for cooperation and good behavior in the classroom.

2. Prepare the faces from the pattern on page 102, using manila, brown, and white paper.

3. Have each child draw his or her face, coloring heavily.

4. Assemble the faces into a class montage.

SEPTEMBER

MATERIALS AND SUPPLIES

- light blue background
- dark blue border and letters
- white paper

- scissors
- broad-tipped colored markers

- colored paper—yellow, dark blue, brown, red, black, green, purple, and orange

INSTRUCTIONS

1. Discuss colors.

2. Prepare the figures from the pattern on page 110. Cut one figure from each of the eight colors.

3. Make 3" by 7" labels from the white paper. Use the broad-tipped markers to print colored letters on the labels.

4. Outline all the items in dark blue marker.

SEPTEMBER

OUR RULES

From *Big Book of Bulletin Boards for Every Month*. Copyright © 2006 Good Year Books.

MATERIALS AND SUPPLIES

- bright orange cloth background
- white typing or computer paper (amount optional)
- transparent tape

- white scrap paper (Used computer paper, clean on one side, is OK.)
- crayons
- scissors

- green border (edge in black if needed)
- green letters (edge in black if needed)
- wide-tipped black and green markers

INSTRUCTIONS

1. With the children, discuss ways to have a quiet, happy classroom. Write their ideas on the chalkboard: Don't make fun of others. Speak quietly. Work quietly. Raise your hand before speaking. Do your best work. Walk quietly in line. Be kind to others. Treat others as you want them to treat you. Be a good neighbor, and so on.

2. Print the rules with black marker on white paper; the number is optional. Outline with green marker.

3. Use the face patterns on pages 105–107. Let each child color a pattern to look like himself or herself and cut it out. (On pages 105–107, two boys' faces have dotted lines added in order to make girls' faces and hair from the same patterns. For girls' faces in these two patterns, omit the ears, if desired.)

4. Outline faces with black marker, if needed.

5. Tape faces on the edges of the bulletin board.

SEPTEMBER

MATERIALS AND SUPPLIES

- dark green background
- white border and letters
- white paper

- colored paper—light blue
- crayons
- scissors

- broad-tipped green marker

INSTRUCTIONS

1. Discuss short vowels.

2. Prepare the big raindrops from the pattern on page 139, using light blue paper.

3. Prepare the duck from the pattern on page 102, using white paper. Add orange feet and beak and a black eye.

4. Prepare the fish from the pattern on page 155. Color it orange.

5. Prepare the hen from the pattern on page 167, using white paper. Add a red face and comb and a yellow beak. Place the hen on a yellow nest.

6. Prepare the cat from the pattern on page 173. Color as desired.

7. Make five 3" by 6" labels from white paper. Use green marker to print the words: cat, hen, fish, drops, and duck.

SEPTEMBER

HOW MANY CATS?
HOW MANY OF EACH COLOR?

MATERIALS AND SUPPLIES

- medium blue cloth background
- orange borders
- black, orange, red, green, blue, purple, yellow, and brown paper (Not all colors are necessary.)
- orange letters
- scissors
- transparent tape

INSTRUCTIONS

1. Prepare a few cats or many cats, depending on grade level. Choose patterns from pages 111 and 112.

2. Place cats on the bulletin board. Tape three around the outside of the bulletin board.

3. Ask the children to count the cats. Then count the number of cats of each color. Older children can write their names and answers on scrap paper and give them to you.

September

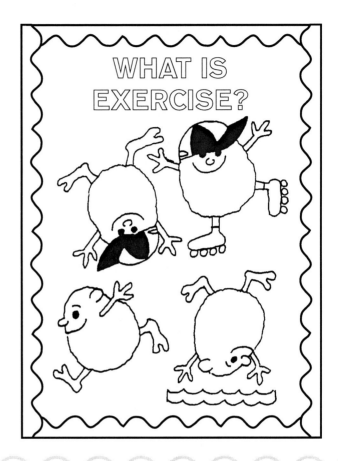

Materials and Supplies

- dark green cloth background
- white border
- white letters
- colored paper (optional)
- transparent tape
- wide-tipped black marker (optional)
- crayons
- scissors
- wide, clear shipping tape
- world map (optional)
- any white paper that crayons can write on (Used computer paper, clean on one side, is OK.)

Instructions

1. Discuss the word exercise with the children. See how many types of exercise they can name. List them on the chalkboard: in-line skating, jumping rope, hopscotch, baseball, basketball, football, bicycling, swimming, aerobics, walking, waterskiing, jumping, running, ballet, and so on.

2. Exercise is important for people of all ages. Discuss the reasons for exercising: to keep your heart and body healthy, to live longer, to have fewer health problems.

3. We exercise from birth, moving arms and legs.

4. Give each child a sheet of paper and let them draw themselves doing one of the exercises listed on the chalkboard.

5. Using the patterns on pages 108–109, 114, and 154 (pattern B), color the Danny Dibby figures, in-line skates, and waves as desired, or use colored paper. Cut them out, tape parts together, and place them on the bulletin board. Tape the children's drawings around the wall.

6. Outline the figures and pictures with marker if needed.

7. If this is a year for summer or winter Olympics, discuss them with the children. Explain that the Olympic games are contests. Those who enter work hard and train for four or more years. Often new records are set. Ask the children what kinds of exercises people compete in: skating, swimming, diving, running, jumping, pole-vaulting, gymnastics, tobogganing, shot-put, skiing, hockey, basketball, track, relay, weight lifting, and so on.

8. There are Olympics for children, Special Olympics for persons with disabilities, and Senior Olympics for older people.

9. Encourage the children to bring pictures of people who enter the Olympics.

10. List the people and in what events they compete.

11. Find the towns and countries of the participants on a map and place dots there. Try to determine how many miles they travel to get to the Olympics. Show on the map where the next Olympics will be held and in what year.

SEPTEMBER

**WE KNOW
WHEN TO CROSS**

From Big Book of Bulletin Boards for Every Month. Copyright © 2006 Good Year Books.

MATERIALS AND SUPPLIES

- yellow background
- black border and letters
- white or manila paper

- colored paper—red, green, and black
- crayons
- scissors

- wide black bias tape (optional)
- broad-tipped black marker

INSTRUCTIONS

1. Discuss safety.

2. Prepare the big figures from the pattern on page 113 (reverse each pattern), press heavily on crayons to color.

3. Prepare the traffic light from the pattern on page 114, using black, red, and green paper.

4. Make the lines from black bias tape or black paper.

5. Outline the figures in black marker.

SEPTEMBER

WHICH ONE ARE YOU?

MATERIALS AND SUPPLIES

- light blue background
- dark blue border and letters
- gray paper (optional)
- white paper
- soda can
- popsicle sticks
- foil
- candy and gum wrappers
- small paper sack
- Styrofoam cup
- straw
- crayons
- scissors
- broad-tipped black marker
- cloth or wallpaper (optional)

INSTRUCTIONS

1. Discuss the problem of litter.

2. Prepare the trash can from the pattern on page 115, using gray paper.

3. Prepare the figures from the patterns on pages 110, 113, or 115–117. Press heavily on crayons to color the figures, or dress the figures in cloth or wallpaper.

4. Prepare the trash; use wrappers and similar materials.

5. Outline all the items in black marker.

13

OCTOBER

MATERIALS AND SUPPLIES

- light blue background
- black border and letters
- white paper
- colored paper—dark blue and black
- scissors
- crayons
- glue
- broad-tipped black marker

INSTRUCTIONS

1. Read about and discuss Columbus.

2. Prepare the figure from the pattern on page 110, using white paper. Color heavily.

3. Prepare the ship from the pattern on page 120, using black paper except for white sails.

4. Prepare the waves from the border patterns on page vii, using dark blue and white paper.

5. Outline the sails, waves, and Columbus in black marker.

OCTOBER

SAIL AWAY WITH BOOKS

MATERIALS AND SUPPLIES

- medium blue cloth background
- black border
- black letters
- transparent tape
- wide-tipped black marker
- crayons
- scissors

INSTRUCTIONS

1. Make a photocopy of the sailing ship and figures on pages 123 and 124. (Do not cut out the ship.) Color the figures as desired.

2. Make the cross red and the water and sky blue.

3. Tape pages 123 and 124 together, making sure the sail lines come together.

4. Outline the entire picture with black marker.

5. Encourage the children to read books, especially stories that took place long ago. Simple biographies of famous people in history are good reading for the children who can read. Spark their interest by reading a simple biography to the class. (See People of Purpose, published by Good Year Books.)

OCTOBER

WHY DO LEAVES CHANGE COLORS?

MATERIALS AND SUPPLIES

- medium blue cloth background
- black border
- black letters
- autumn leaves
- black, yellow, red, orange, and brown paints (optional)
- black, yellow, red, orange, and brown paper (optional)
- any white paper that crayons can write on (Used computer paper, clean on one side, is OK.)
- brown grocery bags (optional)
- wide, clear shipping tape
- transparent tape
- crayons
- scissors
- glue

INSTRUCTIONS

1. Bring colored leaves to class. See if the children can name the trees from which they came.

2. Ask the children why leaves change color in autumn. Trees make chlorophyll in the spring. Chlorophyll makes leaves green. In September or October, trees stop making chlorophyll and the leaves change to other colors.

3. Discuss ways to use colored leaves between two pieces of waxed paper. Press with an iron-on permanent-press setting until the waxed papers fuse together. Use leaves for mulch. Pile leaves in heaps and jump into them. Walk in leaves and listen to them crackle.

4. For a large tree, place together six sheets of 9"-by-12" black paper lengthwise for tree base. Overlap the two black pieces ½" and glue to the bottom end of the tree.

5. As an option, use two large brown grocery bags. Cut down the back seams and cut off the bottoms. Open the two bags and glue the long pieces together at the ends, overlapping 1". Your two glued bags will be about

6' long. Cut a tree base 12" by 24" from another paper bag. Glue it to the tree bottom.

6. As another option, glue three newspaper sections together to make a 6' long strip.

7. Begin at the center top and gradually taper your tree, making it wider at the bottom. Paint the tree black, if needed. Cut it out. Trace around the top half of the tree to use as a pattern for four more branches. Trace around the top half of a branch to make four small branches. Glue branches to the tree.

8. Attach the tree to the bulletin board or wall with shipping tape.

9. Cut leaves from the patterns on pages 121 and 129. Use white paper and crayons, colored paper, or grocery bags painted various colors.

10. Cut a boy's head from the pattern on page 106. From the pattern on page 122, cut the shirt along the broken lines and glue the arms extending out to the sides. Glue the legs and feet to the boy's body. Color.

11. Tape a variety of leaves falling down and in a pile at the boy's feet.

OCTOBER

MATERIALS AND SUPPLIES

- dark green cloth background
- white border
- white letters
- white computer paper (amount optional)

- transparent tape
- crayons
- scissors
- glue

- any white paper that crayons can write on (Used computer paper, clean on one side, is OK.)

INSTRUCTIONS

1. Talk with your class about the meaning of "Good Neighbors." Ask how we can be good neighbors in the classroom. The following are possible subjects for discussion.
   What happens when . . .
   I push my scraps under someone else's desk?
   I interrupt when someone is talking?
   I take things that don't belong to me?
   I am a tattletale?
   I make fun of others?
   I talk back to others?
   I push in front of others in line?
   I treat others the way I want them to treat me?
   I try to keep my things neat?
   I work quietly?

2. Discuss good-neighbor behaviors and add others, if desired.

3. Write all or some of these questions on white paper. Role-play some of the situations written on the paper.

4. Use patterns of children's faces found on pages 103 and 105–107. Color as desired.

5. Patterns for showing anger and sadness in mouths and eyes (front view):
   mouth for sadness, page 106; sad eyebrows, page 107; angry eyebrows, page 106; angry mouth, page 106; angry mouth and angry eyebrows (for side view of face), pages 143 and 170. Cut out each and glue or tape the changes in mouths and eyebrows on top of the expressions already on the faces.

6. Give each child a piece of paper approximately 8" by 10". Ask the children to draw big faces of themselves, choosing an expression, and color it brightly. An option is to give each a pattern of a face to color. Let the children cut them out. Tape these on the wall around the bulletin board.

OCTOBER

MATERIALS AND SUPPLIES

- yellow background
- orange border and letters
- manila or white paper
- glue

- small grocery bags cut to desired size
- crayons
- scissors

- Scotch Magic™ tape
- candy
- broad-tipped black marker
- dress materials (optional)

INSTRUCTIONS

1. Discuss good manners.

2. Prepare the figures from the patterns on pages 113 and 115–117. Dress with cloth as paper dolls, or color heavily with crayons. Outline in marker.

3. Attach candy treats with tape. Glue the bags to the figures' hands.

4. Prepare the balloons (size optional) for the figures' dialogue. Use the black marker to print the words and to outline the balloons. (Add "Thank You" in each balloon.)

OCTOBER

WE BUILD WITH SHAPES

MATERIALS AND SUPPLIES

- medium blue cloth background
- orange border
- orange letters
- glue

- pink, purple, orange, black, yellow, and green paper (optional)
- crayons
- scissors

- any white paper that crayons can write on (Used computer paper, clean on one side, is OK.)

INSTRUCTIONS

1. Prepare bulletin board items from patterns on pages 125–127. Color items heavily or use colored paper.

2. Ask the children to name the shapes in each figure.

3. Point to each item again and let the children count the number of shapes in each.

4. Cut ovals, circles, squares, triangles, rectangles, half circles, quarter circles, diamonds, and so on. Let the children build creative shapes at their tables or desks and glue them on white paper.

OCTOBER

GETTING READY FOR WINTER

MATERIALS AND SUPPLIES

- medium blue cloth background
- black border
- black letters
- black, brown, orange, yellow, and red paper (optional)

- black, brown, orange, yellow, and red paints (optional)
- wide-tipped black marker for labels
- crayons
- scissors
- glue

- felt-tipped black pen
- any white paper that crayons can write on (Used computer paper, clean on one side, is OK.)
- brown grocery bags (optional)

INSTRUCTIONS

1. Ask the children how we get ready for winter. We get out our warm clothes, boots, warm blankets, and so on.

2. Ask the children how animals get ready for winter. Some eat more food with fat in it (nuts and seeds). Many animals grow thicker fur. Birds fluff their feathers on cold days. Some animals store food in underground holes where they sleep. Some animals hibernate (sleep through the cold winter). Squirrels dig holes and bury nuts.

3. Point out that trees and plants also get ready for winter. The leaves change color and drop off so the trees and plants can rest for the winter. Some plants die and new ones come up in the spring.

4. Cut four tree crowns, two orange, one yellow, and one red, from the pattern on page 94. Use colored paper, white paper and crayons, or grocery bags and paints. Place an orange crown on the left and a yellow, a red, and another orange at the right.

5. Cut four brown tree trunks from the pattern on page 98. Use colored paper, white paper colored brown, or grocery bags and paints.

6. Make a brown squirrel (without the dotted line), page 160; a brown and black raccoon, page 128; a brown chipmunk with brown stripes down the back and tail, page 175; and a red or blue bird, page 131. Make the animals with colored paper, white paper and crayons, or grocery bags and paints.

7. Using seed and nut patterns on pages 128 and 158, make a black walnut, light brown hickory nut, dark brown chestnut with light brown center spot, brown acorn, light brown walnut, medium brown hazelnut, black sunflower seeds, and yellow corn. Outline each seed and nut with black pen.

8. Place a yellow or orange strip of paper behind the rows of nuts or seeds to make them more visible.

9. Put acorns, corn, and sunflower seeds on the ground.

OCTOBER

MATERIALS AND SUPPLIES

- yellow background
- black border and letters
- white paper
- colored paper—black

- thin dinner-sized paper plates
- orange and black tempera paints
- small grocery bags

- string
- crayons
- scissors
- glue
- broad-tipped black marker

INSTRUCTIONS

1. Discuss ways we have fun at Halloween.

2. Prepare the tree trunks from the patterns on pages 94 and 131, using black paper.

3. Prepare the ghosts from the patterns on pages 129 or 145, using white paper. Color the eyes and mouths heavily in black. Outline the ghosts in marker.

4. Make the pumpkins by cutting the rims off paper plates and painting the centers orange. Paint black features or add features cut from black paper.

5. Make the owls from small grocery bags. Add yellow eyes, beaks, and feet, black eyes, and brown feathers. Color heavily. Tie feet with string.

6. Make a moon by outlining a whole paper plate in black marker.

OCTOBER

MATERIALS AND SUPPLIES

- light blue background
- black border and letters
- colored paper—red, orange, yellow, brown, and black
- scissors
- glue

INSTRUCTIONS

1. Discuss how leaves change, things to do with autumn leaves, and ways to have fun with fallen leaves.

2. Prepare the tree trunks from the pattern on page 94, using black paper.

3. Prepare the tree crowns from the pattern on page 94, using one red, one brown, two orange, and two yellow sheets of paper. Glue the crowns to the trunks.

4. Prepare small leaves from the pattern A on page 129, using red, orange, yellow, and brown paper. The number of leaves is optional.

November

Materials and Supplies

- light blue background
- black border and letters
- manila or white paper
- scissors

- colored paper—black and light brown
- newspaper or grocery bag (optional)

- crayons
- black tempera paint (optional)
- cotton (optional)

Instructions

1. Talk about Thanksgiving.

2. Prepare the tree trunks from the patterns on pages 94 and 131, using black paper (or a grocery bag or newspaper painted black.

3. Prepare the houses from the pattern on page 130, using light brown paper (or a grocery bag). Color the thatch roof yellow. Color the door and window heavily in black. Color the chimney red.

4. Prepare the table from the pattern on page 135, using light brown paper (or a grocery bag). Cut and glue. Add wood-grain lines.

5. Prepare the figures from the patterns on pages 110, 113, and 115–117, using manila or white paper. Color heavily.

6. Prepare clouds from the pattern on page 172, using white paper or cotton.

7. Prepare the bowls from the patterns on pages 130, 174, and 184. Color as desired.

NOVEMBER

NATIVE AMERICANS

MATERIALS AND SUPPLIES

- light blue background
- brown grocery bags or any brown paper
- tempera paints
- sticks
- manila paper
- crayons
- scissors
- glue
- Scotch Magic™ tape

INSTRUCTIONS

1. Read about Native American tribes, find out why one tribe came to eat with the Pilgrims.

2. Prepare the tepee by gluing together brown paper or grocery bags to form a triangle larger than a small bulletin board. Paint Native American designs on the outside of the tepee, and paint the interior black. Also paint a black line along the open flap.

3. Tape the sticks in place.

4. Prepare the figures from the patterns on pages 110, 113, 115 and 116. The figures shown here are Western Blackfeet Indians. Color the figures heavily. Extend the figures and tepee beyond the borders of the bulletin board and tape, or tape the entire display to a wall.

NOVEMBER

WHY DO WE VOTE?

MATERIALS AND SUPPLIES

- dark blue cloth background
- white border
- white letters

- any white paper that crayons can write on (Used computer paper, clean on one side, is OK.)

- wide-tipped red marker
- scissors
- crayons

INSTRUCTIONS

1. Ask the children why their parents vote. Possible reasons:
   - to elect a new president for our country every 4 years
   - to elect a mayor for our town and other offices
   - to elect people who go to our state capitol to work for our state
   - to elect people who go to Washington, D.C., to work for each of our states

2. In the United States, we are allowed to vote for our leaders.

3. We have two main political parties—Republicans and Democrats.

4. The Democratic party's symbol is a donkey.

5. The Republican party's symbol is an elephant.

6. We need to learn about each candidate before we vote for him or her.

7. Newspapers and television give us information to help us make choices.

8. We go to a voting place to vote. (Explain to the children what people do in a voting place.)

9. Using the patterns on page 136, make a gray elephant and a brown donkey. Color them heavily and cut them out. Color and cut the voting booths and people from patterns on page 127.

10. Glue enough computer sheets together to write these four phrases underneath the pictures, using the red marker:
    to elect a president; to elect other leaders; to decide new laws; to decide how leaders should spend our tax money.

NOVEMBER

MAYFLOWER

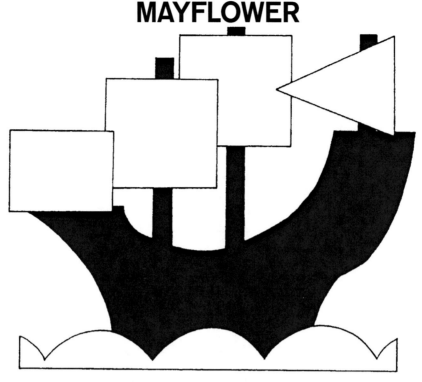

MATERIALS AND SUPPLIES

- black letters
- white paper
- colored paper—black and blue
- tracing paper

- newspapers
- black and white tempera paints
- scissors
- glue

- pencil
- yardstick
- ruler
- broad-tipped black marker
- Scotch Magic™ Tape

INSTRUCTIONS

1. Read about the Pilgrims and the *Mayflower*.

2. Prepare the ship from the pattern on page 120, using black paper for the ship and white paper for the sails.

3. Cut and glue the sails to the masts. Outline the sails with black marker.

4. Using a pencil and ruler, create a 7" by 9" grid of one-inch squares on the tracing paper. There will be 63 squares in all. Lay the grid on the small *Mayflower*.

5. Glue enough newspapers together to cover a 7' by 9' area. Create a grid by marking off the paper into 1' squares. There will be 63 squares in all.

6. Using the small ship and grid as a guide, reproduce the *Mayflower* on the large grid. Duplicate the line(s) you see within each small square in the corresponding large square.

7. Paint the ship black and the sails white.

8. Cut out the ship and tape it to the wall.

9. Prepare the waves (quantity optional) from the border pattern on page vii, using blue paper. Glue in place.

NOVEMBER

READ A BOOK—
ADD A TURKEY FEATHER

MATERIALS AND SUPPLIES

- black cloth background
- orange border
- orange letters
- 10" pie pan or plate
- one sheet of white paper

- red, brown, orange, and yellow construction paper
- straight pins (optional)
- wide-tipped black marker
- thumbtacks (optional)

- staples (optional)
- transparent tape
- crayons
- scissors
- glue

INSTRUCTIONS

1. Develop in children a love for books by reading a short book, a story in a book, or a chapter of a book at the same time each day.

2. Using a 10" pie pan or dinner plate as a pattern, cut one circle from brown paper for the turkey's body.

3. Use the pattern on page 134 and cut from colored paper as many large red, yellow, orange, and brown tail feathers as desired for the children to insert.

4. Glue a tail feather in place at each side of the turkey. Place the turkey on the bulletin board and put thumbtacks or staples at each side next to the feathers.

5. Make a book from a piece of white paper 5" by 7". Fold it in half widthwise and then open it.

6. Make six small wing feathers from the pattern on page 134. Cut red, orange, yellow, or brown feathers. Glue the hand feathers, three on each side, to the turkey's body, with the open book glued to the hand feathers.

7. Using the pattern on page 134, cut head and legs from red paper. Make black eyes and a yellow beak. Make shoes any desired color. Glue head, legs, and shoes in place.

8. Whenever a child reads a book, the child writes his or her name and the book title on a feather. Carefully insert each feather behind the top of the body, between the two glued feathers. If the feathers need to be secured, tape or staple them.

NOVEMBER

MATERIALS AND SUPPLIES

- dark blue cloth background
- orange border
- orange letters
- 2 toy telephones, if possible
- transparent tape

- wide-tipped black marker
- crayons
- scissors
- glue

- any white paper that crayons can write on (Used computer paper, clean on one side, is OK.)

INSTRUCTIONS

1. Discuss ways to talk on the telephone: Say "Hello" when answering the phone. If someone wants to talk to your mother, say, "Just a second, please." Put down the phone receiver quietly and find your mother. Tell her the call is for her. Don't hold the phone in your hand and yell for your mother to come. If your mother can't come to the phone, say, "Can you call back, please?" If you need to write down a caller's number, write it carefully. Say "Thank you" before hanging up the phone. When children call a friend, they should say, "May I talk to Sandy, please?"

2. Using toy telephones, let the children role-play the best way to call someone or answer a phone call.

3. Let some of the children role-play conversations that aren't polite: "Get Joe on the phone," or "I want to talk to Sandy," or "Let me talk to Eric."

4. Encourage the children to comment on the situations and why they are, or aren't, polite.

5. Using patterns on pages 107 and 170, cut out and color the figures, phones, and phone cords. Using the pattern for hands on page 170, cut out and color the hands.

6. Glue or tape phones to faces and add hands.

7. Cut out cartoon "balloons" for conversations and print words with the marker.

NOVEMBER

MATERIALS AND SUPPLIES

- yellow background
- orange and black border
- orange letters
- white paper
- colored paper—brown, red, yellow, and orange
- thin dinner-sized paper plates
- crayons
- scissors
- glue

INSTRUCTIONS

1. Discuss things for which the children are thankful. Have the children draw pictures of these things.

2. Place a black border around each child's picture.

3. Prepare the turkeys from the patterns on page 135. Use a paper plate for the body, or cut one from brown paper. Add feathers and feet made from brown, red, orange, and yellow paper. Glue the head, feathers, and feet to the body.

NOVEMBER

WHAT IS A PUMPKIN?

MATERIALS AND SUPPLIES

- black cloth background
- white border
- orange letters
- yellow, orange, and green paper (optional)
- wide-tipped black marker
- brown grocery bags (optional)
- yellow, orange, and green paints (optional)
- any white paper that crayons can write on (Used computer paper, clean on one side, is OK.)
- transparent tape
- crayons
- scissors
- glue

INSTRUCTIONS

1. Cut orange pumpkins (amount optional) from the pattern on page 137. You can also cut them from white paper and color heavily or cut them from grocery bags and paint them orange.

2. Using the pumpkin vine pattern on page 138, cut from green paper, from the white paper and color heavily, or from grocery bags and paint the parts green.

3. Cut the yellow flower from the pattern on page 138, or cut from white paper and color heavily or from grocery bags and paint yellow. Glue stem, leaf, and flower to the pumpkin.

4. With crayons, color red ridges on the pumpkin.

5. Place one or more pumpkins on the bulletin board and extend parts beyond if desired. (The pumpkin, lower left, is reversed.)

6. Ask the children where pumpkins grow, or assign the question to the children and have them ask their parents.

7. Some pumpkin facts: They are vegetables, grow in patches in fields, are planted in June, ripen in September or October, are used for cattle food, are stringy inside, have many seeds and a tough skin, and have yellow flowers and prickly leaves and stems. They are used for pies (take out the stringy insides and seeds, cut off the tough skin, and cook the thick fleshy part that is left).

8. Cut four sheets of white computer paper in half lengthwise for eight labels. With the marker, write these words:
   a vegetable, tough skin, many seeds, many prickly leaves, yellow flowers, grow in fields, cattle food, pies

NOVEMBER

IS A TURKEY A BIRD?

ONLY BIRDS
HAVE FEATHERS.

MATERIALS AND SUPPLIES

- medium blue cloth background
- brown border
- brown letters
- computer paper
- brown grocery bags (optional)

- wide-tipped black or brown marker
- red, brown, orange, black, and yellow paper (optional)
- red, brown, orange, black, and yellow paints (optional)
- crayons

- scissors
- glue
- any white paper that crayons can write on (Used computer paper, clean on one side, is OK.)

INSTRUCTIONS

1. Do not put the bottom sentence under the turkeys until after the discussion with the children.

2. Discuss this question: Is a turkey a bird? Ask the children what they think and why.

3. Ask children what birds have that no other animals have (feathers).

4. Using white paper and crayons, colored paper, or grocery bags and paints, make three or more turkeys from the pattern on page 139. Make one red, one orange, and one brown. Make as many as your bulletin board can hold, if desired. Glue the legs in place.

5. Overlap the turkeys on the bulletin board.

6. Place two sheets of computer paper end-to-end. Overlap ½" and glue them together. Print these words on it: Only Birds Have Feathers.

7. Let the children draw and color their own turkeys, or give each a pattern to color.

DECEMBER

WHAT IS CHRISTMAS?

MATERIALS AND SUPPLIES

- medium blue background
- black border and letters
- white paper

- broad-tipped black marker
- crayons
- scissors
- glue

- colored paper—light brown, green, yellow, and black construction paper

INSTRUCTIONS

1. Read about and discuss the meaning of Christmas.

2. Prepare the tree trunks and walking staff from the patterns on page 141, using light brown paper.

3. Prepare the manger and stable from the patterns on page 141, using black paper.

4. Prepare the leaves from the pattern on page 154, using green paper. Glue the leaves on the tree trunks.

5. Prepare the figures and angels from the patterns on pages 110, 113, 116, 117, and 141, respectively, using white paper. Color heavily and cut out. Glue the baby in the manger.

6. Prepare the star from the pattern on page 141, using yellow paper.

7. Prepare the sheep from the pattern on page 141, using white and black paper.

8. Outline all the shapes in black marker.

DECEMBER

HOW MANY SYLLABLES?

MATERIALS AND SUPPLIES

- dark blue cloth background
- white border
- white letters
- colored paper (optional)

- glue
- crayons
- scissors

- any white paper that crayons can write on (Used computer paper, clean on one side, is OK.)

INSTRUCTIONS

1. Discuss syllables. (Hold your finger under your chin. For every syllable in a word, your chin goes down, if the word is pronounced correctly.)

2. Prepare these bulletin board patterns: pencil, p. 125; strawberry, p. 96; lemon, p. 153; watermelon, p. 153; turkey, p. 139; candle, p. 144; telephone, p. 107; cantaloupe, p. 144; star, p. 141; squirrel, p. 160; raccoon, p. 128; cheese, p. 168; raspberry, p. 153; tomato, p. 181; banana, p. 153; cupcake, p. 95.

3. Color as desired.

DECEMBER

DECEMBER

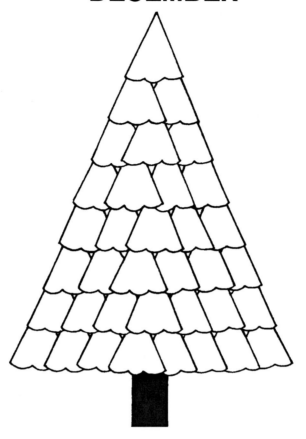

MATERIALS AND SUPPLIES

- white paper
- colored paper (any kind—construction, wrapping, or painted newspaper)—green and black
- colored magazines (optional)
- scissors
- glue
- crayons
- tempera paints (optional)
- Scotch Magic™ Tape

INSTRUCTIONS

1. Read and talk about Christmas.

2. Prepare the crown by cutting 36 triangles or more from the pattern on page 140, using green paper. Glue together at the glue lines, keeping points straight up.

3. Prepare the tree trunk by cutting a 4" by 11" rectangle, using black paper. Glue behind and at the bottom of the assembled crowns.

4. Prepare the ornaments from the pattern on page 140 and 154, using wrapping paper, colored magazine ads, construction paper, or white paper colored heavily.

5. Prepare a star from the pattern on page 141, using yellow paper (tree-top star).

6. Tape the display to the wall.

DECEMBER

MATERIALS AND SUPPLIES

- red cloth background
- white border
- white letters

- crayons
- scissors
- transparent tape

- any white paper that crayons can write on (Used computer paper, clean on one side, is OK.)

INSTRUCTIONS

1. Use any patterns on pages 105–107 to make four faces. Color as desired and cut out.

2. Cut two left tongues and two right tongues from the patterns on page 106. Color them pink and cut them out. Tape them lightly in place with a small piece of tape so they can be removed and the faces used for other bulletin boards.

3. Make the pie and two cakes from the patterns on page 142 and 143. Color and cut them out.

4. Discuss cutting desserts into equal parts. Ask the children if they know how much dessert each child will get to eat.

5. Let the children draw pictures of other things such as twelve cupcakes in a pan, sandwiches on a tray, slices of meat on a plate, cups of milk, or eggs in a frying pan, and divide them equally among the four children pictured on the bulletin board.

DECEMBER

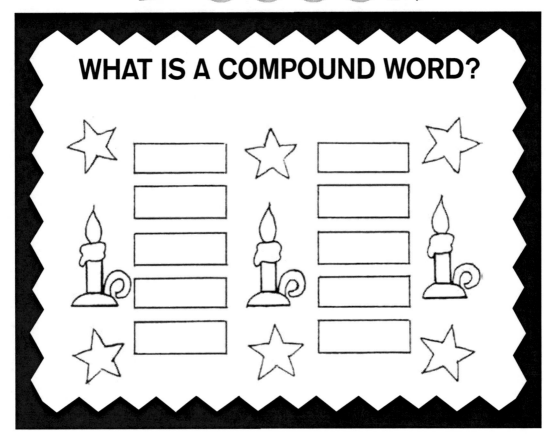

WHAT IS A COMPOUND WORD?

MATERIALS AND SUPPLIES

- black cloth background
- red border
- red letters
- crayons

- white computer paper, amount optional (Used computer paper, clean on one side, is OK.)

- wide-tipped red marker
- scissors

INSTRUCTIONS

1. Discuss with children what a compound word is: a word that is made up of two or more parts that are words themselves.

2. Prepare words for the bulletin board, number optional. Cut computer sheets in half lengthwise. Write one compound word on each half sheet. Use a wide-tipped red marker.

3. Make stars and candles from the patterns on pages 141 and 144. Use yellow for stars, and color candles red with yellow flames and white holders. Color heavily and then cut out the items. Arrange them on the bulletin board and around the room.

DECEMBER

HANUKKAH: HOW WE CELEBRATE

MATERIALS AND SUPPLIES

- dark blue background
- gold wrapping (or yellow) paper for border and letters
- manila or white paper
- colored paper—gold or yellow
- light brown paper, wood grain contact paper, or grocery bag
- white cloth
- wrapping paper
- ribbon
- crayons
- glue
- scissors
- Scotch Magic™ Tape

INSTRUCTIONS

1. Discuss Hanukkah. Have the children write or draw pictures about the holiday.

2. Prepare the table from the pattern on page 135, using light brown paper, wood-grain contact paper, or a grocery bag.

3. Prepare the tablecloth from the pattern on page 145, using white (or any color) paper or cloth.

4. Prepare the menorah from the pattern on page 131, using gold or yellow paper.

5. Prepare the dishes from the patterns on pages 130, 174 and 184, using manila or white paper. Color heavily.

6. Prepare the figures from the patterns on pages 110, 113, and 115–117, using manila or white paper. Color heavily.

7. Prepare the packages by cutting wrapping paper and ribbon. Box sizes are optional. Glue or tape the ribbons to the wrapping paper.

8. Prepare the dreidel from the pattern on page 184, using manila or white paper. Color heavily.

DECEMBER

OUR FIVE SENSES: CAN YOU NAME THEM?

MATERIALS AND SUPPLIES

- dark green background
- white and red borders
  (offset with red behind white)
- white letters
- manila and white paper
- colored paper—yellow,
  light blue, red, and light brown
- crayons
- scissors
- broad-tipped black marker
- grocery bag (optional)

INSTRUCTIONS

1. Discuss the five senses.

2. Prepare the face from the pattern on page 145, using manila or light brown paper or a grocery bag. Color heavily.

3. Prepare the star from the pattern on page 141, using yellow paper.

4. Prepare the cookie from either pattern A or B on page 182, using light brown paper or a grocery bag. Decorate as desired. Color heavily.

5. Prepare the candy cane from the pattern on page 146, using white paper. Color heavy red stripes.

6. Prepare the hand from the pattern on page 182, using manila or light brown paper or grocery bag. Color heavily.

7. Prepare the water drops from the pattern on page 139, using light blue paper.

8. Prepare the bell from the pattern on page 146, using red paper.

9. Outline all the shapes in marker.

10. Add white paper strips to connect eyes, ears, nose, hand, and tongue to star, bell, cookie, raindrops, and candy cane, respectively.

DECEMBER

WHAT IS A SUPERMARKET?

MATERIALS AND SUPPLIES

- dark blue cloth background
- yellow border
- yellow letters
- jar or can labels
- cash register receipts (optional)

- pictures of grocery items from store ads or newspaper ads
- wide-tipped black marker
- crayons
- scissors

- glue
- any white paper that crayons can write on (Used computer paper, clean on one side, is OK.)

INSTRUCTIONS

1. From the pattern on page 152, color and cut out the boy and shoes. Glue the shoes to the boy's legs on the dotted lines. (Omit the boy's right arm.)

2. Use the pattern on page 134 for the cart. Color and cut it out.

3. Ask the children what supermarkets have. List their responses on the chalkboard.

4. Let the children draw pictures of people working in a supermarket.

5. Ask the children to bring in jar or can labels from things that were bought at a supermarket, as well as cash register receipts (optional), pictures from grocery ads, or newspaper ads.

6. Put pictures, labels, and so on, on and around the bulletin board.

7. Let the children role-play jobs that workers perform in a supermarket. As each performs, let the rest of the class guess what job he or she is acting out.

DECEMBER

SOME TREES STAY GREEN: WHY?

MATERIALS AND SUPPLIES

- medium blue cloth background
- black border
- black letters
- any white paper that crayons can write on (Used computer paper, clean on one side, is OK.)

- black, yellow, and green colored paper (Several shades of green are preferable so the trees will stand out individually.)
- large brown grocery bag (optional)
- newspapers (optional)

- black, yellow, and green paints (optional)
- wide-tipped black marker
- wide, clear shipping tape
- a 6" saucer or a 10" plate
- crayons
- glue

INSTRUCTIONS

1. Ask the children if there are trees that don't change colors or lose their leaves in autumn. Evergreen trees have dark green needlelike leaves and stay green all winter. In the spring new, light green needlelike leaves begin to appear at the end of each dark green cluster of leaves, so the leaves are always green.

2. Cut black tree trunks from the pattern on page 140 (number optional).

3. Using the pattern for tree crowns on page 156 (patterns A and B), fold the paper and cut two kinds of crowns. One has straight lines and the other, from the optional dotted-line pattern, has pointed sides. If you use white paper for crowns, color the crowns different shades of green–light to very dark–for variation. As an option, cut crowns from colored paper, brown grocery bags, or newspapers, and make them different shades of green.

4. Glue trunks in place.

5. Outline each tree with black marker, if needed, so it stands out from the others.

6. Cut a yellow sun by tracing around a 6" saucer or a larger plate.

7. To make a very large tree crown for the wall of your classroom, cut open six large brown grocery bags down the back seams and cut off the bottoms. Open the bags and glue the six bags together, overlapping each ½".

8. Cut a triangular crown from the top center down to each corner. The tree crown will be 6' tall and 4' wide at the bottom. Paint it green.

9. Cut a trunk 6" wide and 16" long. Paint it black. Glue the trunk to the bottom of the tree, overlapping ½".

10. Tape the tree to the wall with the wide tape.

DECEMBER

MATERIALS AND SUPPLIES

- dark green background
- white border and letters
- white paper
- wrapping paper

- colored paper—light brown, light green, yellow, and red
- ribbon
- Scotch Magic™ Tape

- gold or silver paper (optional)
- scissors
- crayons

INSTRUCTIONS

1. Read and talk about holidays and their symbols.

2. Prepare cookies from pattern A or B on page 182, using light brown paper. Color heavily.

3. Prepare the dreidel and candy cane from the patterns on pages 184 and 146, using white paper. Color heavily.

4. Prepare the angel and Santa from the pattern on page 110, using white paper. Color heavily.

5. Prepare the star from the pattern on page 141, using yellow paper.

6. Prepare the sheep from the pattern on page 141, using white paper and black paper.

7. Prepare the packages by cutting flat shapes from wrapping paper (sizes optional) and taping on ribbons.

8. Prepare the bells from the pattern on page 146, using red paper.

9. Prepare the tree from the pattern on page 140, using light green paper for the crowns and black for the trunk.

10. Prepare the manger from the pattern on page 141, using light brown paper.

11. Prepare the baby Jesus and pancakes from the patterns on pages 141 and 184, respectively, using white paper. Color with crayons.

12. Prepare the menorah from the pattern on page 131, using yellow, gold, or silver paper.

December

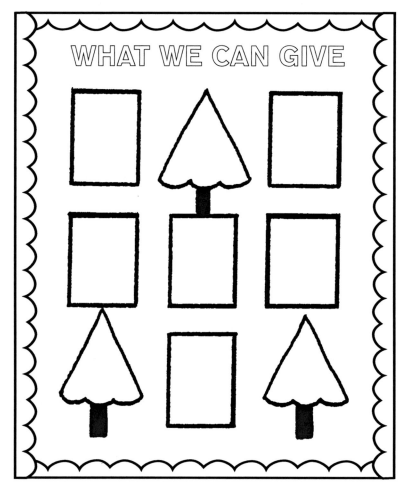

WHAT WE CAN GIVE

MATERIALS AND SUPPLIES

- red background
- white border and letters
- white paper (lined or unlined)
- colored paper—black and green
- crayons
- scissors
- glue
- glitter (optional)
- yellow or gold paper for menorahs (alternate option)

INSTRUCTIONS

1. Discuss ways we can give of ourselves rather than buying gifts for loved ones. Allow the children to write about their ideas or to draw pictures.

2. Prepare the tree trunks from the pattern on page 140, using black paper.

3. Prepare the crowns from the pattern on page 140, using green paper. Glue the crowns on the tree trunks. Add ornaments from the pattern on page 140.

4. As an alternate option, prepare the menorahs from the pattern on page 131, using yellow or gold paper.

JANUARY

MATERIALS AND SUPPLIES

- light blue background
- black border (points turned out toward wall) and letters
- white and manila paper
- colored paper—black and dark blue newspapers (optional
- broad-tipped black marker
- crayons
- scissors
- black and blue tempera paints (optional)

INSTRUCTIONS

1. Discuss winter.

2. Prepare the tree trunks from the patterns on pages 94 and 131, using black paper or newspaper painted black.

3. Prepare the ice by cutting an oblong shape (size optional) from dark blue paper or newspaper painted blue.

4. Prepare the figures from the patterns on pages 110, 113, 115, 116–118, and 119, using manila or brown paper. Color heavily.

5. Prepare the sled from the pattern on page 147. Color heavily.

6. Prepare the snowman and snowball from the patterns on pages 140, 154, and 176, using white paper. Glue the parts of the snowman together.

7. Prepare the tree snow, using white paper. Cut to fit.

8. Outline all shapes in black.

JANUARY

BIRDS: DO THEY GET COLD?

MATERIALS AND SUPPLIES

- light blue cloth background
- red border
- red letters
- red, orange, and black paper
- 3 sheets of white computer paper
- wide-tipped black marker
- crayons
- scissors

INSTRUCTIONS

1. Prepare the red cardinal from the pattern on page 148. Use red paper. Color an orange beak, a black eye with orange around it, a black face, black boots, and orange scarf and earmuffs, and a black headband. Outline wing with black pen.

2. Read about birds. They keep cool in summer and warm in winter. Birds are warm-blooded. Eating more food in winter helps them keep warm. Fluffing their feathers also keeps them warm in winter. In summer they flatten their feathers to keep cool.

3. We can help birds in winter by regularly feeding them sunflower seeds and birdseed. Supply fresh water and tiny gravel stones to help them digest their food.

4. Let the children color birds from the pattern on page 148, or draw their own.

5. Use three sheets of computer paper and write these labels: warm-blooded, fluff feathers for warmth, eat more in winter for warmth. Use a wide-tipped marker for making letters and a black border around each paper.

From *Big Book of Bulletin Boards for Every Month.* Copyright © 2006 Good Year Books.

JANUARY

BIRDS FOR BOOKS

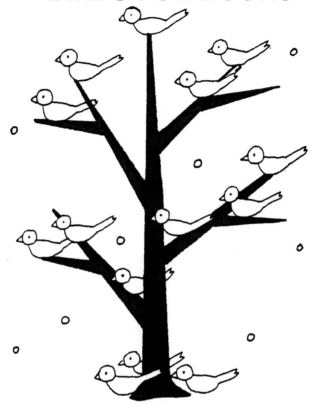

MATERIALS AND SUPPLIES

- black letters
- black paper
- colored paper
- brown grocery bags (optional)

- paints (optional)
- cotton balls (optional)
- wide, clear shipping tape
- crayons
- transparent tape

- any white paper that crayons can write on (Used computer paper, clean on one side, is OK.)

INSTRUCTIONS

1. Using the bird pattern on page 156, cut as many birds as desired. Use white paper and color the birds. Cut them out, or use colored paper. Put the birds in a box on the table.

2. Encourage the children to read library books by adding a bird for each book read. Have each child write his or her name on a bird and the book title on the front when they finish a book.

3. Assemble the large tree from the October directions on page 16. Cut out the tree from black paper, or use grocery bags and black paint. Tape it to the wall with wide, clear shipping tape.

4. From the pattern on page 147, cut snowflake A or B from white paper, or else use cotton balls. Tape them to the wall.

5. Tape the birds to limbs and smaller branches.

JANUARY

CONCENTRATION GAME

MATERIALS AND SUPPLIES

- black cloth background
- orange border
- orange letters
- eight 5" by 8" cards

- bulletin board space within reach of children
- 16 letter-sized envelopes, 3½" by 6½"

- 32 thumbtacks
- crayons
- scissors
- glue

INSTRUCTIONS

1. Use the patterns on page 149 for the boy, hand, and question mark. Color and cut.

2. Turn the flaps of the letter-sized envelopes backward and glue them to the back of the envelope.

3. Tack the envelopes to the bulletin board (two tacks at the top of each). Place them on the lower part of the bulletin board in two, three, or four rows so the children can reach them.

4. Cut the 5" by 8" cards in half so each is 4" by 5".

5. Print eight sets of matching words on the sixteen cards.

6. Write important words from any subject you want to reinforce, including health, science, reading, spelling, and social studies.

7. For kindergarten, match pairs of colors, numbers, beginning sounds, and so on.

8. Mix your sixteen words (eight matching pairs) and place one word in each of the sixteen envelopes. Turn the cards so only the blank sides show.

9. Divide your class into two teams. Let a child from one team come up and turn any two cards around. Hold them up for the class to see where they are located in there envelopes. If the two cards match, the child gets a point for his or her team. The matching cards are then placed in envelopes so the class can see the words. If the two cards do not match, the child puts them back in the two envelopes, with the blank sides showing.

10. A child from the other team comes up and turns any two cards around. Continue this procedure until all the cards are matched.

11. The team with the most pairs matched is the winner. Repeat the same game or use eight new sets of words.

12. If eight sets of words are too many, use fewer sets for each game.

JANUARY

Materials and Supplies

- medium blue cloth background
- black border
- black letters
- 6 sheets of white computer paper (for the calendar)
- wide-tipped black marker
- black felt-tipped pen
- black paper
- any white paper that crayons can write on (Used computer paper, clean on one side, is OK.)
- crayons
- scissors
- glue
- yardstick
- pencil

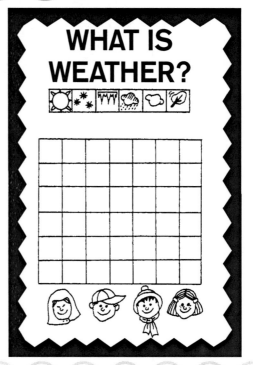

WHAT IS WEATHER?

Instructions

1. To make a calendar with 3" squares for a month, place six computer sheets together (three above and three below), without overlapping. Tape the adjoining edges together.

2. Turn the taped paper over so the taped sides are on the back.

3. With a yardstick and pencil, begin at the left side and mark off every 3" across the top and bottom. Connect the dots from top to bottom with the felt-tipped pen. (There will be leftover paper at the right.)

4. Starting at the top, mark off every 3" down both sides. Connect the dots. (There will be leftover paper.)

5. Count off seven rows at the top. Cut off the extra paper.

6. Count down six rows on the sides. Cut off the extra paper. You now have a calendar with seven rows across for seven days, and six rows down for six weeks. (Some months require six rows when the first day is on a Friday or Saturday and there are 31 days.)

7. With the wide marker, print the dates in the proper places for January.

8. Choose and color four faces only, from patterns on

pages 105–107. To represent four kinds of weather, add a cap, page 109; a rain hat, page 150; and a scarf and wool hat, page 150. The fourth figure represents warm, sunny weather (no hat), page 105. Color and tape the figures in place.

9. Prepare weather symbols from the patterns on page 150. Color the sun yellow with orange points. Color the upper part of the rain cloud dark blue. Color the tree in the wind as desired.

10. Cut out the letters for the word January, or print them on white paper. Place them above the calendar.

11. Ask the children what they think weather is. It is what is happening in the air around us. It changes from day to day.

12. Ask the children how many of their parents watch the weather report on TV or listen to it on the radio.

13. Let the boys and girls tell you what time of the year the symbols represent. Also, ask what time of year they like best and why.

14. Ask the children to check the newspaper or television for the next day's weather report daily for one month. Tape the predicted weather symbol on the bulletin board calendar. See how many predictions come true. Continue for every day of January.

JANUARY

SLEEP: WHY DO
WE NEED IT?

MATERIALS AND SUPPLIES

- dark blue background
- light blue border and letters
- manila, brown, or white paper

- crayons
- scissors
- broad-tipped black marker
- dark blue paper (optional)

From *Big Book of Bulletin Boards for Every Month.* Copyright © 2006 Good Year Books.

INSTRUCTIONS

1. Read about and discuss rest and sleep.

2. Prepare the sleeping face from the pattern on page 164, using brown, manila, or white paper. Color heavily.

3. Make four 4" by 24" labels from white paper. Cut dark blue letters or print the words on the labels with a broad-tipped marker.

JANUARY

MATERIALS AND SUPPLIES

- black background
- white border
- white letters
- colored paper (optional)

- white paper pieces (for the "juggling" path)
- crayons
- scissors
- glue

- any white paper that crayons can write on (Used computer paper, clean on one side, is OK.)

INSTRUCTIONS

1. Ask the children to name as many fruits as they can. Write them on the chalkboard: apples, apricots, avocados, bananas, blackberries, blueberries, cantaloupes, cranberries, dates, elderberries, grapes, grapefruit, kiwi, lemons, mangos, oranges, papayas, peaches, pears, pineapples, plums, raspberries, rhubarb, star fruit, strawberries, tangerines, watermelons

2. Talk about the importance of eating fruits each day for good health.

3. Ask the children to name favorite fruits and why they like them.

4. Discuss things made from fruits: juices, jams, sauces, pies, dried fruit, sherbet, ice cream, jellies, fruitcake, salads, cookies, and so on.

5. Using the patterns on pages 153, 154, 101, 96, and 144, cut fruits from scrap computer paper and color heavily, or use colored paper.

6. Use the boy pattern on page 152. Color as desired and glue shoes on legs at dotted lines. Use white paper for the "juggling path" between plums.

7. Bring in a variety of fruits. Cut them in half. Study the seeds. Offer children samples to taste (of course, first check with parents concerning food allergies).

49

JANUARY

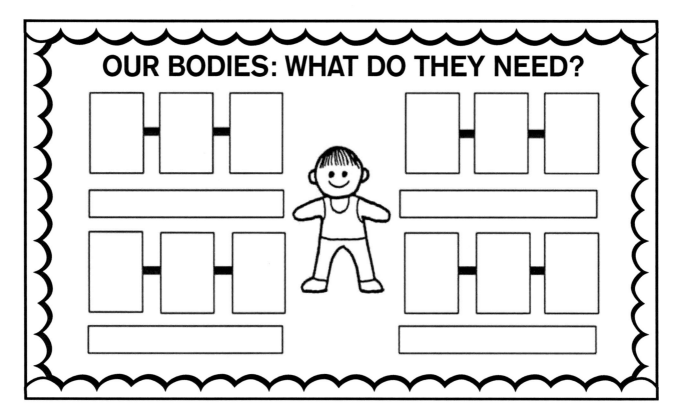

OUR BODIES: WHAT DO THEY NEED?

MATERIALS AND SUPPLIES

- light blue cloth background
- white and dark blue borders (dark blue border placed so that it shows beyond white border)
- dark blue letters
- white paper
- brown paper (optional)
- scissors
- crayons
- glue
- broad-tipped black and dark blue markers
- magazine ads
- dark blue bias tape or paper

INSTRUCTIONS

1. Discuss the body's needs for a proper diet, emphasizing the four food groups.

2. Prepare the figure from the pattern on page 110, using white or brown paper. Color heavily. Outline in black.

3. Make the word labels by cutting four 4" by 16" strips of white paper. Use the dark blue marker to print the following words on the labels: meats, nuts; milk, cheese; fruits, vegetables; and cereals, bread. Outline each label.

4. Add connecting lines made from strips of dark blue paper or bias tape.

5. Cut out colored magazine pictures of foods and glue them on twelve sheets of 9" by 12" white paper.

JANUARY

WHAT IS SNOW?

MATERIALS AND SUPPLIES

- dark blue cloth background
- yellow border
- yellow letters
- brown, red, yellow, and white paper
- brown grocery bag (optional)

- cotton or cotton balls (optional)
- transparent tape
- paints (optional)
- crayons
- scissors

- glue
- any white paper that crayons can write on (Used computer paper, clean on one side, is OK.)

INSTRUCTIONS

1. Talk about snow. Read a snow story such as A Snowy Day by Ezra Keats.

2. Ask the children if they know where snow comes from. Water droplets (vapor) high in the air form ice crystals of different shapes that fall to the ground as snow.

3. Prepare a snow strip as wide as the bulletin board and approximately 8", or more, deep. Use white paper, cotton, or grocery bags painted white.

4. Cut a barn from the pattern on page 151. Use red paper with black windows; use white paper and color it dark red and black; or use a grocery bag painted red with black windows. Add white paper or cotton or a grocery bag painted white for snow on the barn roof.

5. Make a yellow house from the pattern on page 151. Cut black windows and a red door and roof from colored paper, or use white paper colored heavily or a painted grocery bag. Add paper or cotton snow.

6. From the pattern on page 95, cut a brown tree trunk and branches; use white paper and color it brown; or use a grocery bag and brown paint. Add paper or cotton snow.

7. Using the pattern on page 151, cut a fence from red paper, white paper colored red, or a grocery bag painted red. Add paper or cotton snow.

8. Cut snowflakes from white paper using the snowflake pattern A on page 147, or use cotton balls.

JANUARY

WHAT IS A THERMOMETER?

MATERIALS AND SUPPLIES

- dark blue cloth background
- white border
- white letters
- wide-tipped black marker
- transparent tape
- red paper (optional)
- crayons
- scissors
- glue
- any white paper that crayons can write on (Used computer paper, clean on one side, is OK.)

INSTRUCTIONS

1. Talk about thermometers and what they are used for: to measure air temperatures inside and outside, to tell when meat is done or when candy reaches certain temperatures, to measure body temperatures, to tell how hot the water is in a swimming pool, and so on.

2. Heat causes the mercury in the thermometer tube to rise higher.

3. Ask the children how they feel when the temperature outside is high and the air is hot. How do they feel when it is very cold and the temperature is low?

4. What time of the year is hot? cold? Not too hot or too cold?

5. To make a thermometer, glue enough white papers together for a strip 48" long and 7" wide. With a black marker, make two long black lines, 1" apart, from the top, continuing down the center to within 1½" of the bottom. Glue a 5" round circle of red paper, or white paper colored bright red, at the bottom of the thermometer, still leaving 1½" below. Beginning at the red ball, draw black temperature lines across the thermometer every 3" until you reach the top. The bottom line can be −20°; the next one −10°; and so on. Continue by 10s until you reach 110° F at the top.

6. For the mercury tube, cut a red strip of paper 1" wide and 6" long, or any desired length. Attach the bottom of the strip to the red ball.

7. Fold the top of the red strip at the place where the predicted temperature is for the day, adding additional red strip as needed.

8. To cut icicles, fold used computer paper in half lengthwise. Draw two short icicles about 3" long, and one about 7" long.

9. Use face patterns from pages 103 and 105–107 (trace the face on page 103 and reverse it). Make four mittens from the pattern on page 143. Make button mouths, with the space around them, for the two side figures from the pattern on page 100 and tape them on lightly. Earmuffs and scarf patterns are on pages 110 and 150. The hat pattern is on page 148. Tape the hats on lightly. Eyes looking down are on page 103. The serious mouth for the boy with the scarf is on page 143. Tape it to his face lightly.

10. The children can report to the class temperature readings in other parts of the country or the world.

FEBRUARY

BE MY VALENTINE

MATERIALS AND SUPPLIES

- red letters
- red and black paper
  or newspapers

- red and black tempera
  paints (optional)
- scissors

- glue
- Scotch Magic™ Tape

INSTRUCTIONS

1. Discuss Valentine's Day.

2. Prepare the trees from the patterns on pages
   132 and 133 (smaller tree trunk), using black
   paper or newspapers painted black. Glue the
   branches to the trunks (smaller branches).

3. Prepare the big hearts from the pattern on
   page 155, using red paper or newspapers
   painted red. Glue to the trees.

4. Tape the display to the wall.

FEBRUARY

MATERIALS AND SUPPLIES

- dark blue cloth background
  transparent tape
- crayons
- scissors

- white letters
- white border
- wide-tipped black marker

- white computer paper
  (Used computer paper,
  clean on one side, is OK.)

INSTRUCTIONS

1. Ask the children to think of safety rules we all should follow. Write them on the chalkboard: Wear seat belt. Look both ways before crossing the street. Keep both hands on the handlebars of a bicycle. Remove toys from steps. Keep away from moving swings. Keep wet hands away from electric light switches. Don't tease dogs you don't know. Keep hands inside moving cars. Learn to swim. Bicycle with care. Don't talk to strangers. Don't play with matches. Be aware of things that can be poisonous in your home, and don't touch or taste them.

2. Print some safety rules on white computer paper and put them on the bulletin board.

3. Color and cut out safety items from these patterns:
   girl and road, p. 119; water drops, pattern A p. 139; boy and electric switch, p. 157; dog, p. 158, boy in water, p. 157; car and steps, p. 159; seat belt, p. 157.

4. Let the children draw safety pictures. Outline them with marker and tape them to the wall.

FEBRUARY

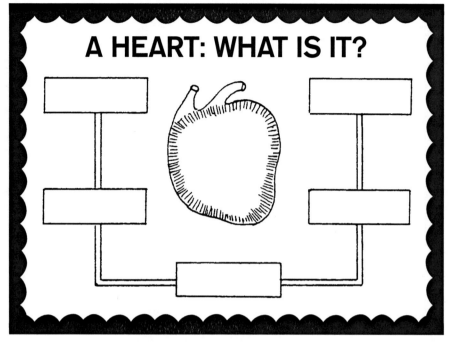

A HEART: WHAT IS IT?

MATERIALS AND SUPPLIES

- red cloth background
- pink border
- black letters
- pink paper

- 5 sheets of white computer paper
- crayons

- scissors
- glue
- wide-tipped black marker

INSTRUCTIONS

1. Discuss the heart with children. Before birth, when you were only 1" long, your heart was beating. The heart is a pump. The heart sends blood through tubes called veins and arteries. (Look at your hands and arms for blood vessels.) The heart sends oxygen and food to the body cells. The heart is located in the center of your chest. There are two pumps coming from the heart. About 2 ½ quarts of blood are pumped through a child's heart every minute. In one year a child's heart pumps nearly 1,000 gallons of blood. People's hearts are about the size of a fist. Healthy foods help your heart stay well.

2. Cut three sheets of computer paper in half lengthwise for labels. With a black marker, write these words on five labels: pump, beating, veins; arteries, oxygen; chest, fist, healthy foods; 2½ quarts, 1,000 gallons.

3. Foods low in fat help our hearts stay healthy. Vegetables, chicken, fish, fruits, whole-grain breads and cereals, and skim milk help your heart stay well.

4. Cut a heart from the pattern on page 156. Color it darker pink around the edge and white in the center. Outline it with black marker.

5. Connect the labels with pink paper strips 1" wide.

FEBRUARY

MATERIALS AND SUPPLIES

- red cloth background
- white border
- white letters
- crayons
- scissors
- glue

- a child's book of George Washington to read to the children (for example, the picture book *George Washington: Father of Our Country* by David Adler)

- any white paper that crayons can write on (Used computer paper, clean on one side, is OK.)
- wide-tipped black marker

INSTRUCTIONS

1. From patterns on pages 160 and 161, prepare the figures of George Washington and a boy talking to him, asking him questions. For the boy's face, reverse the pattern on page 103 and add the arm on page 170. Color heavily as desired and glue arms to the figures.

2. Outline the figures in marker, if needed.

3. Prepare the "balloon" from white paper. Print the words: "Hello, Mr. Washington. May I please ask you a question?"

4. Tell the children that you are going to read them the story of George Washington's life. Ask them to listen carefully, because when you are finished reading, you will choose someone to be Mr. Washington. Then the boys and girls will ask the chosen person a question about things they heard in the story. "Mr. Washington" will try to answer questions as if he or she really were George Washington. Remind children to address the person playing Mr. Washington with respect by saying "Mr. Washington, may I please ask you a question?" Choose as many children to act the part of Mr. Washington as you desire. Each "Mr. Washington" could answer three or four questions before you choose another child to play Mr. Washington. Continue as long as interest is sustained.

FEBRUARY

SHADOWS: WHY DO WE HAVE THEM?

MATERIALS AND SUPPLIES

- light blue background
- dark blue border and letters
- white paper
- colored paper—yellow, green, red, orange, gray, and brown
- glue
- crayons
- scissors
- broad-tipped black marker

INSTRUCTIONS

1. Discuss shadows, especially in regard to Groundhog Day (February 2).

2. Prepare the figure from the pattern on page 110 or 117, using white or brown paper. Color heavily.

3. Prepare the trees from the patterns on pages 94, 141, and 154. Use brown paper for the trunks and green paper for the crowns. Glue the crowns to the trunks.

4. Prepare the bell from the pattern on page 146, using red paper.

5. Prepare the candy cane from the pattern on page 146, using white paper. Color in heavy red stripes.

6. Prepare the cat from the pattern on page 173, using brown, black, gray, or orange paper.

7. Prepare the big heart from the pattern on page 155, using red paper.

8. Prepare the sun from the pattern on page 154, using yellow paper.

9. Make the shadows by drawing around each object on gray paper and cutting out the shapes.

10. Outline all the shapes in black marker.

FEBRUARY

WHAT IS A RAIN FOREST?

MATERIALS AND SUPPLIES

- medium blue cloth background
- black border
- black letters
- colored paper (optional)
- crayons with as many shades of green as possible
- transparent tape
- scissors
- glue
- any white paper that crayons can write on (Used computer paper, clean on one side, is OK.)

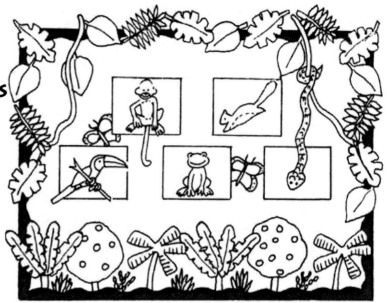

INSTRUCTIONS

1. Ask children if they know what a rain forest is.

2. What does the word *rain* tell us about this kind of forest?

3. A rain forest has warm weather all year and lots of rain.

4. Get a children's book about rain forests from the library. Two good books are *The Great Kapok Tree* by Lynne Cherry and *Tropical Rainforests* by Gail Gibbons. Read the chosen book to the children and show them the pictures.

5. Rain forests have very tall trees. Many grow to be 250' high. (To illustrate this, draw a 1" high orange tree on the chalkboard, representing a 10' high orange tree. Twenty-five inches above the top of your orange tree is where a rainforest tree would stand in comparison. This is as tall as a 25-story skyscraper.) These tall trees are the upper canopy of the forest.

6. Smaller trees, such as orange, banana, and palm trees form the lower canopy of trees, along with the vines and plants. Very little light reaches the floor of the rain forest.

7. Most rain forests are located near the equator. Point to the equator on a map. That is the warmest part of the world.

8. Many animals live in rain forests: bats, alligators, sloths, flying squirrels, parrots, sunbirds, toucans, hummingbirds, golden frogs, lizards, snakes, deer, antelope, butterflies, spider monkeys, and so on.

9. Make these animals from patterns: tan flying squirrel, p. 160 (using the dotted lines); green snakes with black scales, p. 98; yellow frog, brightly colored butterflies, and toucans, p. 162 (black body, yellow beak and face, orange around the blue eyes, blue legs, patch of red underneath the tail, and brown twig); spider monkey and tail, p. 126.

10. Make trees and plants from patterns and color them various shades of green for contrast: dark green orange tree (follow dotted lines), orange fruit, p. 128; trunk, p. 140; green banana leaves, p. 104 (four for each tree), and green trunk, p. 140; palm leaves, p. 162, and trunk, p. 141; brown vine, p. 158; green plant leaf, p. 121 (follow dotted lines); dark green snake plant with leaves edged in yellow, p. 162; green Christmas cactus, p. 162; rain forest leaf, p. 104.

11. Let the children draw and color rain-forest animals or color the patterns of the animals. Tape the animals around the outside of the bulletin board.

FEBRUARY

PETS: HOW WE CARE FOR THEM

MATERIALS AND SUPPLIES

- yellow background
- red border and letters
- manila or white paper
- crayons

- glue
- broad-tipped red marker
- writing paper (optional)
- pet feed

- plastic sandwich bags
- string
- Scotch Magic™ Tape

INSTRUCTIONS

1. Read about and discuss care of pets.

2. Prepare the following pets, using manila or white paper. Color heavily with any colors desired.
   - turkey (from pattern on page 135)
   - small sheep (from pattern on page 141)
   - rabbit (from pattern on page 147)
   - bird (from pattern on page 163)
   - dog and cat (from pattern on page 173)
   - hamster, turtle, fish (from patterns on page 155)
   - hen (from pattern on page 167)
   - pig (from pattern on page 165)
   - snake (from pattern on page 176)
   - duck (from pattern on page 102)

3. Make up small bags of pet feed, tie them closed, and attach to the pictures with tape.

4. As an optional activity, ask the children to write about proper pet care. Glue their reports to the bottoms of the pictures.

5. Outline all the sheets of paper in red marker.

FEBRUARY

WHOM DO WE LOVE?

MATERIALS AND SUPPLIES

- yellow background
- red border and letters
- colored paper—red
- crayons
- scissors
- glue

INSTRUCTIONS

1. Talk about love and the people, pets, and other things we love. Ask the children, "How do we show love?"

2. Prepare the big hearts from the pattern on page 155, using red paper. The number of hearts is optional.

3. Give the children white paper and have them color pictures of people, pets, and other things they love. Tell the children to color heavily and then to cut out and glue their pictures on the hearts.

MARCH

CAN YOU SEE THE WIND?

MATERIALS AND SUPPLIES

- light blue background
- dark blue border and letters
- manila or white paper
- colored paper—brown, black, and yellow
- crayons
- glue
- doll clothes
- heavy cord
- clothespins
- pins
- broad-tipped black marker

INSTRUCTIONS

1. Read the poem "Who Has Seen the Wind?" by Christina Rosetti. Ask students to think about the wind and what it does.

2. Prepare the tree trunk and leaves from the patterns on pages 94 and 129 pattern A, respectively, using black and brown paper.

3. Prepare the figures from the patterns on page 117, using manila or white paper. Color heavily and cut out.

4. Prepare the house from the pattern on page 163, using yellow paper. Add black windows and doors, red chimney, and brown roof. Color heavily.

5. Prepare the kite from the pattern on page 164, using white paper. Color heavily and glue on string.

6. Prepare the smoke from the pattern on page 163, using black paper.

7. Pin a length of heavy cord in place for the clothsline.

8. Attach doll clothes to the cord with clothespins. Pin the clothes at an angle to make it appear as if they are blowing in the wind.

MARCH

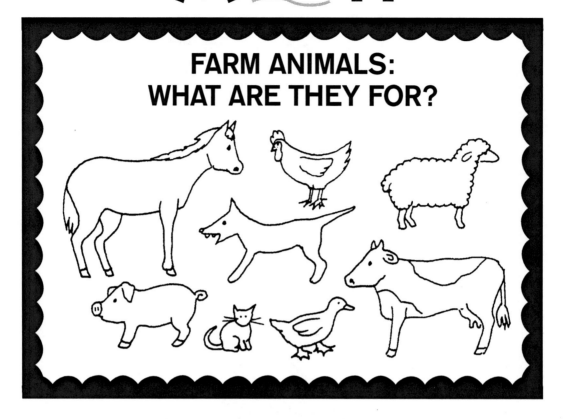

**FARM ANIMALS:
WHAT ARE THEY FOR?**

MATERIALS AND SUPPLIES

- medium blue cloth background
- black border

- black letters
- crayons
- scissors

- any white paper that crayons can write on (Used computer paper, clean on one side, is OK.)

INSTRUCTIONS

1. Ask the children to name as many farm animals as they can and tell what each is used for:

   cow—milk (cattle for meat)
   horse—work
   duck—food
   sheep—wool, meat
   chicken—meat, eggs
   pigs—meat
   cat—work (catches mice)
   dog—work (guards property, herds sheep)

2. Cut animals from patterns on pages 165, 166, 138, and 158. Color animals and cut them out: black-and-white cow, pink pig, brown horse, white sheep with black face and legs, brown chicken, white duck with orange bill and feet, orange cat.

3. Let the children make farm animals on white paper or color patterns.

MARCH

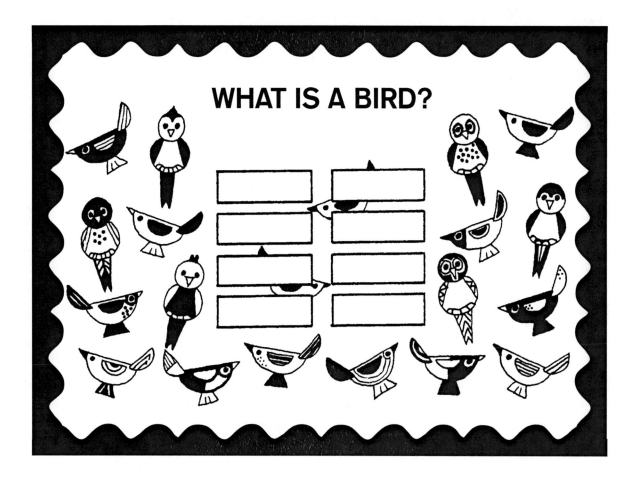

MATERIALS AND SUPPLIES

- light blue cloth background
- dark blue border and letters
- manila and white paper

- crayons
- scissors
- glue
- broad-tipped blue marker

INSTRUCTIONS

1. Read about birds.

2. Prepare birds from the patterns on pages 147 and 163, using manila paper. Color heavily and cut out.

3. Make the labels by cutting eight 4½" by 9" strips of white paper and printing the following words in dark blue marker (or cutting and gluing dark blue letters): head, body, bones, feathers, eyes, beak,, wings, and tail. Outline the labels in dark blue marker.

MARCH

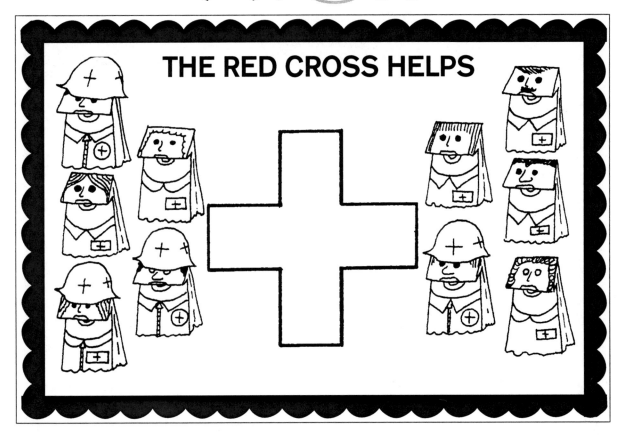

THE RED CROSS HELPS

From *Big Book of Bulletin Boards for Every Month*. Copyright © 2006 Good Year Books.

MATERIALS AND SUPPLIES

- green background
- red border, reversed, and letters
- small paper sacks

- white paper
- red paper
- crayons
- scissors

- glue
- newspaper (optional)
- red tempera paint (optional)

INSTRUCTIONS

1. Read about and discuss what Red Cross workers do.

2. Make the workers from paper sacks. Color in the hair, eyes, and top of mouth on each sack bottom. Color in the bottom of the mouth and chin on the side of the sack. Below each chin, color in a blue dress or jumpsuit.

3. Prepare the protective helmets from the pattern on page 167, using white paper. Add red crosses; then glue to heads (sack bottoms).

4. Prepare the large cross, using red paper or newspapers painted red. The size of the cross is optional.

5. Cut small pieces of white paper for the name tags. Add red crosses; then glue on sacks.

MARCH

MILK: WHERE DOES IT COME FROM?

MATERIALS AND SUPPLIES

- medium blue cloth background
- green border

- green letters
- crayons
- scissors

- any white paper that crayons can write on (Used computer paper, clean on one side, is OK.)

INSTRUCTIONS

1. Make a cow from the pattern on page 165. Color it black and white. Give it a pink nose.

2. Make a barn and fence from the patterns on page 151. Color them red.

3. For the grass, use the pattern on page 169. Color it green.

4. From the patterns on page 169, make a truck and dairy. Color the tires black, the cab dark blue. Color the dairy building brown.

5. From the pattern on page 168, make a milk jug. Color the cap green. Make swiss cheese and color it yellow. Make an ice cream carton and color the lid purple and the letters purple. Make a yogurt cup and color it green. Make a box of butter. Color it yellow. Cut them out.

6. Ask the children where milk comes from. Milk comes from cows. (Many people in the world also get milk from goats, sheep, camels, llamas, reindeer, and water buffaloes.) Milk is an almost perfect food. It is very good for your health. It makes strong bones and teeth. Dairy cows give milk. Most dairy cows are black-and-white Holsteins. They live on farms and eat grass, hay, and corn. Farmers put the milk in tanks to keep it cold. The milk is pumped out of the farmer's tanks and into a tank truck. The truck takes the milk to dairies, where it is put into jugs and delivered to stores.

7. Some milk is made into cheese, yogurt, butter, and ice cream.

8. Let each child draw a cow, color it, and cut it out or else make one from a pattern and color it. A barn and many cows can be a farm scene.

MARCH

WHY DO TEETH COME

CROWN

ROOTS

MATERIALS AND SUPPLIES

- dark green cloth background
- white border
- white letters
- 5 computer sheets

- thumbtack
- wide-tipped black marker
- transparent tape
- crayons
- scissors

- any white paper that crayons can write on (Used computer paper, clean on one side, is OK.)

INSTRUCTIONS

1. Ask the children if they know when and why our baby teeth come out. Teeth facts: At about six or seven years of age, the roots of the baby teeth dissolve gradually and the teeth fall out. The permanent teeth grow in to fill each space left by the baby teeth.

2. Encourage brushing teeth, drinking milk, and eating good food so permanent teeth stay healthy.

3. Using the patterns on page 106, color and cut out the faces. On page 106, cut out the mouths with missing teeth. Attach the mouths to the faces with a small piece of tape.

4. Make one large tooth from the pattern on page 116. Use black marker to outline the tooth. Glue the tooth on a sheet of paper, and

with the marker, write the words crown and roots around the tooth.

5. Write these sentences on the computer sheets:
   Roots of baby teeth dissolve.
   Baby teeth fall out.
   Permanent teeth grow in.
   Teeth have crowns and roots.

6. Use narrow white paper strips above and below the tooth picture. Secure the two glued paper strips with a thumbtack at the top. Glue the ends behind the tooth picture. Glue another paper strip at the back of the tooth picture and continue the strip to the border at the bottom of the bulletin board.

MARCH

MATERIALS AND SUPPLIES

- yellow background
- dark green border, reversed, and letters
- white paper
- colored paper—dark green
- crayons
- scissors
- glue
- broad-tipped green marker

INSTRUCTIONS

1. Read about or discuss St. Patrick. Explain that he was a missionary to Ireland, winning over many people to Christianity. In the United States, St. Patrick's Day is celebrated on March 17 with parades and people wearing green to honor Ireland.

2. Prepare the figure from the pattern on page 110, using brown paper (the probable color of his coat). Color heavily.

3. Prepare the shamrocks from the pattern on page 164, using green paper. Cut four leaves, overlap them slightly, and glue to the stem. For a 3-D effect, bend the centers on the dotted lines.

4. Cut strips of white paper for the labels. Size is optional. Use green marker to outline the labels and to print the words Missionary to Ireland.

MARCH

MATERIALS AND SUPPLIES

- dark green background
- orange border and letters
- white paper
- colored paper—light brown
- crayons
- scissors
- glue
- broad-tipped black marker

INSTRUCTIONS

1. Discuss fire and the ways fire is good and bad.

2. Prepare the logs from the pattern on page 171, using brown paper. Color heavy brown graining.

3. Prepare the flames from the pattern on page 171, using yellow paper. Add an orange tip to each flame. Glue the flames together.

4. Make 4" by 12" labels from white paper. Use orange marker to outline the labels and to print good and bad aspects of fire on them.

APRIL

WHY DO WE HAVE EASTER?

MATERIALS AND SUPPLIES

- medium blue background
- dark green border and letters
- white paper
- colored paper—brown, green, and dark green
- crayons
- glue
- newspapers (optional)
- brown tempera paint (optional)
- writing or drawing paper

INSTRUCTIONS

1. Discuss the meaning of Easter. Have the children write or draw pictures about the holiday.

2. Make the cross from brown paper or newspaper painted brown. Draw in wood-grain lines. Make the horizontal bar 7" by 24", the vertical bar 7" by 31". Glue the bars together.

3. Prepare the flowers from the pattern on page 113, using green and white paper. Color in orange stamens.

4. Offset dark green paper behind the children's writing or drawings.

APRIL

MATERIALS AND SUPPLIES

- light blue background
- dark green border and letters
- white paper
- scissors

- colored paper—various shades of light green, pink, yellow, black, brown, and dark blue
- colored magazines (optional)

- wallpaper (optional)
- pink and yellow tissue paper (optional)
- glue
- broad-tipped black marker

INSTRUCTIONS

1. Discuss spring.

2. Prepare the tree trunks from the pattern on page 94, using black or brown paper or wallpaper.

3. Prepare the crowns from the pattern on page 94, using shades of light green paper or wallpaper.

4. Prepare the little flowers from the pattern on page 158 (pattern A), using pink and white paper or colored magazine ads, wallpaper, or crumpled tissue paper. Glue the flowers to each other and to the trees.

5. Prepare the raindrops and clouds from the patterns on pages 139 (pattern A or B) and 172, respectively, using dark blue paper.

6. Prepare the bird and nest from the patterns on pages 147 and 174, respectively, using white paper. Color heavily. (Reverse the bird pattern on page 174.)

APRIL

EASTER: A SPECIAL TIME

MATERIALS AND SUPPLIES

- orchid or white background
- purple border and letters
- colored paper—brown, yellow, and purple
- manila paper
- broad-tipped purple marker
- crayons
- scissors
- writing paper (optional)
- white chalk

INSTRUCTIONS

1. Discuss Easter customs. Have the children write or draw pictures about Easter. Outline their papers in purple marker. Display children's artwork beyond the bulletin board boundaries. Outline each with a purple marker.

2. Prepare the eggs from the pattern on page 174. Color heavily.

3. Prepare the rabbits from the pattern on page 147, using brown paper. Use chalk to make the white of the eye and a black crayon to make the center and outer edge. (Reverse some of the rabbit patterns.)

4. Prepare the chicks from the pattern on page 96, using yellow paper. Add orange feet and beaks and black eyes. (Reverse some of the chick patterns.)

5. Offset purple paper behind the children's writing or drawings on the bulletin board.

APRIL

MATERIALS AND SUPPLIES

- medium blue cloth background
- black border
- black letters
- brown grocery bags (optional)

- green paint (optional)
- green, brown, yellow, and red paper (optional)
- transparent tape
- crayons
- scissors

- glue
- any white paper that crayons can write on (Used computer paper, clean on one side, is OK.)

INSTRUCTIONS

1. For grass, use green paper or brown grocery bags painted green. Length and width of grass is optional.

2. Prepare a barn from the pattern on page 151. Color it red or use red paper. Color windows black. From the pattern on page 151, make a yellow house. Color windows and roofs black and the door red, or use colored paper.

3. From the pattern on page 95, cut a bare tree and color it brown, or use brown paper. Cut a tree crown from page 95. Color it green or use colored paper. Glue or tape crown to tree trunk.

4. Cut two red fences from the pattern on page 151. Cut dark blue clouds and raindrops from pages 151, 172, and 139 (size optional), or use white paper and color them dark blue.

5. Add colored flowers from the pattern on page 151.

6. Ask the children which things need water from the rain: gardens, animals, farmers' fields, flowers, grass, trees, people, forests, mountains, lakes, and so on.

7. Ask the children what happens when there is not enough rain: grass and plants turn brown, fish die when rivers dry up, the ground turns to dust, farmers lose their crops, and so on.

8. Raindrops fall from dark clouds. The larger the drops, the faster they fall.

9. Discuss what happens when there is too much rain: floods, good ground washes away, crops and trees wash away, homes are destroyed, and so on. (Show pictures from web sites and books.)

APRIL

MATERIALS AND SUPPLIES

- medium blue background
- dark blue border and letters
- white and manila paper
- colored paper—light brown and dark blue
- scissors
- crayons
- glue
- broad-tipped black marker
- wallpaper and writing paper (optional)

INSTRUCTIONS

1. Discuss Passover. Have the children write or draw pictures about the holiday.

2. Prepare the figures from the patterns on pages 113 and 116, using manila paper. Color heavily. (Reverse the figure on page 113 to make the man.)

3. Prepare the table from the pattern on page 135, using light brown paper or wallpaper.

4. Prepare the tablecloth from the pattern on page 145, using white paper. Color as desired.

5. Prepare the matzos from the patterns on page 174. Color as desired.

6. Prepare the book from the pattern on page 174. Color heavily.

7. Outline all the shapes in black marker.

8. Offset sheets of dark blue paper behind the children's writing or drawings.

APRIL

MATERIALS AND SUPPLIES

- light blue background
- black border and letters
- white paper

- colored paper—brown, red, black, yellow, and green
- crayons

- scissors
- glue
- broad-tipped black marker

INSTRUCTIONS

1. Read about and discuss animal babies.

2. Prepare the hen from the pattern on page 167, using white paper. Add a red comb and face and a black eye. Place the hen on a yellow nest.

3. Prepare the sheep from patterns on pages 141 and 146, using white paper. Color in heavily black legs and face.

4. Prepare the bears from the pattern on page 172, using brown paper. Add black eyes.

5. Prepare the bird from the pattern on page 147, using red paper. Add a yellow beak and legs and a black eye.

6. Prepare the tree trunk from the pattern on page 94, using black paper.

7. Prepare the bird nest from the pattern on page 174, using brown paper. Make the birds red. Glue the nest in the tree.

8. Prepare the turtles from the pattern on page 155, using brown and black paper.

9. Prepare the chicks from the pattern on page 96, using yellow paper. Add orange legs and beak and a black eye. (Reverse the chick pattern.)

10. Prepare the cat from the pattern on page 173. Color heavily.

11. Prepare the kittens from the pattern on page 97. Color heavily.

12. Prepare the dog and puppy from the patterns on pages 173 and 172, respectively. Color heavily.

13. Outline all the shapes in black marker.

APRIL

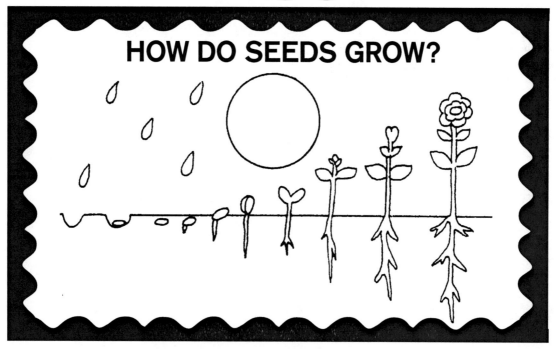

HOW DO SEEDS GROW?

MATERIALS AND SUPPLIES

- medium blue cloth background
- dark green border (Outline with black marker, if needed.)

- dark green letters
- brown grocery bags
- colored paper
- felt-tipped black marker
- crayons
- scissors

- glue
- any white paper that crayons can write on (Used computer paper, clean on one side, is OK.)

INSTRUCTIONS

1. Make a brown seed, the stages of seed growth, and the sun from the patterns on pages 100, 149, and 154. Color heavily and cut them out.

2. From the patterns on page 168, make a yellow-and-orange flower and brown roots. Glue them together at the dotted lines.

3. Make the brown earth from paper bags. Cut the back seam open and cut off the bottom of each bag. Make the earth long enough to reach across your bulletin board and wide enough for the longest flower roots. Glue parts of bags together to make them the right size.

4. Outline each item with black marker, if needed.

5. Use the pattern on page 139 to make white raindrops.

6. Make a sun from the pattern on page 154.

7. Ask the children if they have ever planted seeds. Let them tell about their experiences.

8. Explain the stages of seed growth and what seeds need.

9. If desired, give each child a polystyrene foam cup (with a hole in the bottom for drainage). Add potting soil and let the children plant seeds. (Tomato plants are simple to grow. Take seeds from a healthy tomato and plant them in the soil, about $1/4$" deep. Keep them moist, but not too wet, and out of direct sunlight for a couple weeks.)

APRIL

UMBRELLAS AND RAINCOATS IN APRIL: WHY?

MATERIALS AND SUPPLIES

- medium blue cloth background
- black border
- black letters
- wide-tipped black marker
- dark blue paper for clouds (optional)
- transparent tape
- crayons
- Scissors
- glue
- any white paper that crayons can write on (Used computer paper, clean on one side, is OK.)

INSTRUCTIONS

1. Using the patterns, color and cut out seven figures from pages 96–101. Make seven raincoats from page 170, five rain hats from page 150, six boots from page 101, and two umbrellas and handles (three parts) from page 161. Color heavily with bright colors and cut the pieces out. Glue two parts of the umbrella handle together at the dotted line. Glue the handle to the umbrella top at the dotted line. Tape or glue rain hats and coats on the figures. Make white rain drops from the pattern A or B on page 139 and tape them to the bulletin board.

2. Ask the children why umbrellas and raincoats are good to have in April. Teach the rhyme:
   April showers
   Bring May flowers.

3. Umbrellas have been used for many hundreds of years. They used to be made from oiled cloth and wood. In ancient Egypt only rich people were allowed to have them. Rich ladies in England, many years ago, carried silk umbrellas trimmed with pretty lace.

4. Let the children draw and color themselves in raincoats or with umbrellas. As an option, give children a pattern and let them color it brightly. Place figures on the bulletin board and around the outside.

5. Outline pictures with marker, if needed.

APRIL

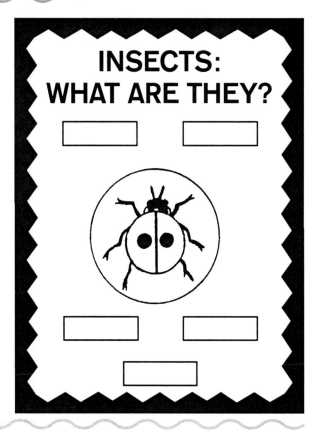

INSECTS: WHAT ARE THEY?

MATERIALS AND SUPPLIES

- yellow cloth background
- red border
- red letters
- encyclopedias, web sites, and books showing pictures of insects
- one dinner plate
- black, red, and yellow paper (optional)
- any white paper that crayons can write on (Used computer paper, clean on one side, is OK.)
- computer paper
- wide-tipped black marker
- crayons
- scissors

INSTRUCTIONS

1. Make a ladybug from the pattern on page 175. Use colored paper or white paper and color it heavily: red wings with two black spots. Make a black stripe, black legs, black eyes, a black head, and black antennae. Make three yellow spots on two sides and the back of the head. Cut out the bug. Outline the three yellow spots on the head with black marker.

2. Using yellow paper, trace around a dinner plate with wide black marker. Cut out the circle, including the black border, and place it behind the ladybug.

3. Show the children pictures of insects. Use the encyclopedias, web sites, or a children's book about insects, such as Amazing Insects by L. A. Mound or Bug Wise by Pamela Hickman.

4. Discuss insects. They are often small, with three pairs of legs, a segmented body (three parts), and usually two pairs of wings and two antennae.

5. Insects include the bee, ant, cockroach, termite, mosquito, cricket, wasp, ladybug, moth, dragonfly, flea, butterfly, firefly, walking stick, louse, and fly.

6. Insects live nearly everywhere on earth. You find them from snowy places to deserts.

7. Some insects make noises. Some insects get air (or breathe) through holes in their sides.

8. Some insects bite animals and people.

9. Insects are many colors.

10. Insects are food for birds, fish, and other animals.

11. Use three sheets of computer paper, cut in half lengthwise, to make five labels. Write with marker: six legs; body in three parts; usually two pairs of wings; usually two antennae; food for animals.

APRIL

MATERIALS AND SUPPLIES

- orange cloth background
- yellow border
- yellow letters
- black paper
- crayons
- scissors

- pictures of things recyclable: steel and aluminum cans, plastic, paper, glass containers, tires, used motor oil, and old cars
- clear plastic bags
- aluminum soda cans

- newspaper
- pins or staples
- any white paper that crayons can write on (Used computer paper, clean on one side, is OK.)

INSTRUCTIONS

1. From face patterns on pages 105–107, choose two girls' faces and two boys' faces. Color heavily and cut them out.

2. Using the hand pattern on page 170, color and cut out five hands.

3. Make a tire by tracing around a dinner plate on black paper. Cut out the center.

4. Fold a page or two of newspaper so it fits beneath the boy's hand. Use straight pins or staples to hold the newspaper in place.

5. Use four or five plastic bags to pin or staple beneath the first girl's hand.

6. Place several used aluminum soda cans in a plastic bag and pin or staple it in place under the hand.

7. Pin or staple the tire above two hands.

8. Discuss recycling: the process of making new things from used things instead of throwing them into landfill holes in the ground.

9. We can help by recycling trash, such as cans, glass, and paper, as much as possible.

10. We must never throw trash on the ground.

11. Ask the children to watch for trash that is thrown on the ground. Do not ask them to pick things up. They are simply to make lists of what they see and share the lists with the class.

12. Let the children help you find pictures of recyclable items and put them on the bulletin board.

13. After the children bring in their lists of items thrown on the ground, let them draw pictures of these things. Put the pictures outside of the bulletin board, on the wall.

MAY

A FARM IS . . .

MATERIALS AND SUPPLIES

- light blue background
- black and green border
- black letters
- paper plate
- white and manila paper

- colored paper—red, yellow, gray, black, green, brown, orange, pink
- wide green rickrack
- cotton (optional)

- crayons
- scissors
- glue
- broad-tipped black marker

INSTRUCTIONS

1. Read about and discuss farms.

2. Prepare the house from the pattern on page 151, using yellow paper for the main structure. Add a gray roof and windows and a red door and chimney. Color heavily.

3. Prepare the trees from the pattern on page 94, using black and green paper. Glue the parts of the tree.

4. Prepare the pig from the pattern on page 177, using pink paper. Add black eyes and nostrils.

5. Prepare the sheep from the pattern on page 141, using white paper. Add black faces and legs.

6. Prepare the figures from the pattern on page 117, using white or brown paper. Color heavily.

7. Prepare the barn from the pattern on page 178, using red paper. Add a black door and gray roof.

8. Prepare the corn from the pattern on page 176, using green paper.

9. Prepare the cow from the pattern on page 176. Color as desired.

10. Prepare the clouds from the pattern on page 172, using white paper or cotton.

11. Prepare the birds from the pattern on page 131 or 147. Color as desired.

12. Make the grass from green rickrack.

13. Prepare the small turkey from the pattern on page 135, using a paper plate and brown, red, yellow, and orange paper.

14. Prepare the ducks from the pattern on page 138, using white paper. Add orange feet and bill and a black eye.

15. Prepare the chicks and the sun from the patterns on pages 96 and 154, respectively, using yellow paper. Add black eyes to the chicks.

16. Outline all the shapes in black marker.

MAY

VEGETABLES: BELOW AND ABOVE

MATERIALS AND SUPPLIES

- medium blue cloth background
- dark green border
- dark green letters
- brown grocery bags (for soil)

- 6 sheets of computer paper cut in half lengthwise
- crayons
- scissors
- glue

- any white paper that crayons can write on (Used computer paper, clean on one side, is OK.)
- black felt-tipped pen

INSTRUCTIONS

1. There are many tiny parts to these items, so you can cut them out and leave a white border around each, if desired. Color each item heavily.

2. Use the pattern on page 148 and color the carrot orange. Stems, roots, and leaves are green.

3. Make a potato plant using the pattern on page 150. Color stems and leaves green, and roots brown.

4. Use the radish pattern on page 152. Color the radish red, stems and leaves green, and roots brown.

5. The turnip pattern is on page 97. Color the top of the turnip purple, the bottom white. Leaves and stems are green. Roots are brown.

6. The red beet pattern is on page 152. Color the beet dark red, the leaves green and red, the stems red, and the roots brown.

7. The pepper plant is on page 158. Color the pepper red. (When green peppers are left on the vine, they eventually turn red and are much sweeter.) Color the stems and leaves green, and the roots brown.

8. Use the green bean plant pattern on page 175. Color the beans, stems, and leaves green, , and the roots brown.

9. Use the lettuce pattern and roots on page 161. Color the lettuce pale green and the roots brown, and glue the roots to the bottom of the lettuce at the dotted line. Outline the vegetable and underground roots with black marker.

10. Make a tomato plant from the pattern on page 185. Color the tomatoes red, the stems and leaves green, and the roots brown.

11. If desired, outline all the vegetables, leaves, stems, and roots with black marker.

12. Using one or more large brown grocery bags, make a strip of soil as deep as desired.

13. Cut a yellow sun by tracing around a saucer or plate.

14. Ask the children to name as many vegetables as they can. Write them on the chalkboard. Ask if the vegetables grow above or below ground. Stress the importance of eating vegetables daily for good health. Let the children tell you what their mothers make from vegetables: salads, mixed vegetables, vegetable casseroles, soups, and so on.

15. Let the children color vegetable patterns or draw their own vegetables.

16. Put a name label under each vegetable on the bulletin board, if desired.

MAY

WHAT IS A FLOWER?

MATERIALS AND SUPPLIES

- dark blue background
- light blue border and letters
- white paper
- colored paper—yellow and two shades of light green
- crayons
- scissors
- glue
- broad-tipped blue marker

INSTRUCTIONS

1. Read about flowers.

2. Prepare the flower from the pattern on page 177, using yellow paper for the petals. Color the stamens and pistil orange. Use two shades of green for the stem and the leaves. Glue the parts of the flower.

3. Make seven 3" by 8" labels from white paper. Use a dark blue marker to print the words: stamen, pistil, receptacle, petal, stem, sepals, and leaf.

4. Add strips of white paper as lines between the flower parts and the labels.

MAY

MATERIALS AND SUPPLIES

- dark blue cloth background
- white border
- white letters
- crayons

- scissors
- glue
- wide-tipped black marker

- any white paper that crayons can write on (Used computer paper, clean on one side, is OK.)

INSTRUCTIONS

1. From the patterns on page 179, color the woman's head, arm, and hand. Cut and tape them together (so the head can be used again).

2. Make a boy's head and neck only, reversed, from the pattern on page 103. Add an arm from page 170. Color and tape them together.

3. Make a white "balloon." Write the words with a the wide marker.

4. Discuss the importance of saying "thank you" at home and at school, or anywhere someone does something for you.

5. Let the children tell you when saying "thank you" is appropriate: when someone does something for us or gives us something. Some of those who help us are the school lunch workers who serve us our food, our teacher who gives us something, the librarian who hands us books, the bus driver who stops to let us off at our home or a bus stop, and cashiers who serve us at stores. Many times each day we say "thank you" to those who do something for us or help us, and we can add a smile too. Mothers and fathers do more for us than anyone and they like to hear those two words also.

6. Let the children make simple thank-you letters for their mothers and fathers. Tell them thank you for their care. List things such as cooking food, washing clothes, cleaning the house, mowing the lawn, washing the car, fixing things, working so we can have a home.

7. If children can't write, let them draw "thank-you" pictures showings things their parents do for them.

8. The children can draw pictures of things for which they need to tell others "thank you." Put these on the bulletin board.

JUNE

WHAT IS SUMMER?

MATERIALS AND SUPPLIES

- light blue background
- dark green border and letters
- white or manila paper
- colored paper—yellow, black, green, brown, and dark blue
- crayons
- scissors
- glue
- broad-tipped black marker

INSTRUCTIONS

1. Read about and discuss summer.

2. Prepare the figures from the patterns on pages 115–118, using white or brown paper. Color heavily.

3. Prepare the trees from the patterns on page 94, using green and black paper. Glue the tree parts.

4. Prepare the waves from the pattern on page vii, using dark blue and white paper. Glue together.

5. Prepare the skateboard from the pattern on page 118. Color heavily. Glue to the figures or pin to the bulletin board.

6. Prepare the sun from the pattern on page 95, using yellow paper.

7. Prepare the basketball from the pattern on page 118, using brown paper.

8. Prepare the hoop from the pattern on page 118. Color as desired.

9. Prepare the book from the pattern on page 174. Color as desired. Glue the book to the figure.

10. Prepare the doll from the pattern on page 118. Color as desired. Glue the doll to the figure.

11. Outline all the shapes in black marker.

JUNE

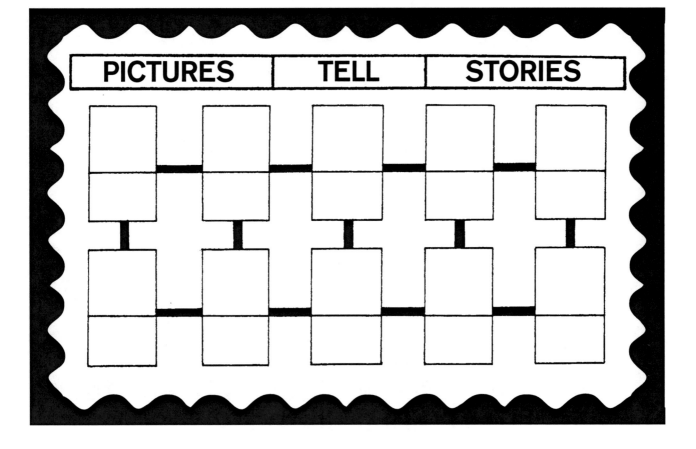

PICTURES   TELL   STORIES

MATERIALS AND SUPPLIES

- light blue background
- dark blue border and letters
- pictures from magazines or newspapers (ones that will inspire writing)
- white paper

- writing paper
- pencils
- broad-tipped dark blue marker
- strips of dark blue paper to separate stories

INSTRUCTIONS

1. Glue the pictures on white paper, and then display the pictures at the top of each paper. Give the children time to think about the pictures and to make up stories about what they see. Then have them write their stories.

2. Attach the children's stories to the bottoms of the pictures. Outline the pictures and stories in blue marker. Display. Place remaining stories on the wall beyond the bulletin board borders. Outline each with dark blue marker.

JUNE

MY FAVORITE PLACE

MATERIALS AND SUPPLIES

- dark green cloth background
- white border, edged with orange marker
- white letters, edged with orange marker
- wide-tipped orange marker
- crayons
- scissors
- transparent tape
- any white paper that crayons can write on (Used computer paper, clean on one side, is OK.)

INSTRUCTIONS

1. Using the pattern on page 149, make the boy and hand and question mark. Color as desired. Tape the hand lightly in place.

2. Ask the children to tell about a favorite place where they like to go: a comfortable room or chair, the library, a friend's house, or their grandparents' house; or an outdoor place, such as a porch swing, pool, ballpark, tree house, or fishing spot.

3. Give the children each a piece of paper. Let them draw themselves in their favorite place, doing what they enjoy most. Outline each scene with orange marker.

4. If the children can write, let them write about their favorite place and draw a picture of it.

5. Display the children's pictures and writing on the bulletin board. Tape extras on the wall.

85

JUNE

MATERIALS AND SUPPLIES

- orange background
- dark green border and letters
- manila or white paper

- colored paper—dark green
- crayons
- scissors
- writing paper (optional)

INSTRUCTIONS

1. Have the children write about or draw pictures about happy times and sad times.

2. Prepare the faces from the patterns on pages 105–107, using manila, white, or brown paper. Color heavily.

3. Prepare sad eyebrows and sad mouths from patterns on pages 106 and 107.

4. Offset sheets of dark green paper behind the children's writings or drawings.

JULY

MATERIALS AND SUPPLIES

- light blue background
- dark blue border and letters
- white paper
- crayons
- scissors
- glue
- broad-tipped blue marker

INSTRUCTIONS

1. Read about Uncle Sam (information can be found in encyclopedias or on Web sites), and discuss what he represents.

2. Prepare Uncle Sam from the patterns on pages 180 and 181, using white paper. Color heavily so that the white hat has a blue band with white stars, the tie and mouth are red, the coat and eyes are blue. Glue the hat in place.

3. Outline the shapes in dark blue marker.

4. Make six 3" by 7" and one 3" by 14" labels from white paper. Use a dark blue marker to outline each label and to print on the 3" by 7" labels: United, States, Nickname, Symbol, 1812, and U.S. On the 3" by 14" label print: Colors of Our Flag.

MATERIALS AND SUPPLIES

- light blue background
- dark blue border and letters
- manila, brown, or white paper
- crayons
- scissors
- glue
- broad-tipped black marker

INSTRUCTIONS

1. Talk about Independence Day.

2. Prepare the figures from the patterns on pages 110, 113, and 115–117, using brown, white, or manila paper. Color heavily.

3. Prepare the flags from the pattern on page 181. Color red, white, and blue.

4. Prepare the instruments from the patterns on pages 181 and 116. Color heavily.

5. Prepare the fireworks from the pattern on page 183. Color heavily.

6. Outline all the shapes in black marker.

JULY

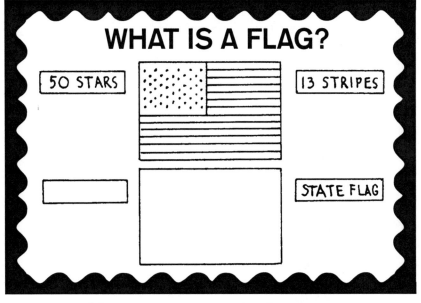

WHAT IS A FLAG?

50 STARS

13 STRIPES

STATE FLAG

MATERIALS AND SUPPLIES

- light blue cloth background
- dark blue border
- dark blue letters
- An American flag
- a state flag (optional)

- 2 sheets of computer paper
- crayons
- scissors
- wide-tipped black marker

- any white paper that crayons can write on (Used computer paper, clean on one side, is OK.)

INSTRUCTIONS

1. Display the U.S. flag. Give each child a flag pattern to color or let each make his own (p. 182).

2. Place the flag of your state under the U.S. flag, or let the children each make one and choose one for the bulletin board.

3. Make four labels from two sheets f computer paper cut in half lengthwise. Print with the marker: fifty stars, thirteen stripes, color your state flag. Describe it in two words.

4. Ask the children why our country's flag is important: The flag is a symbol of our country and of freedom. We honor it because we are free to choose jobs, homes, religion, and leaders for our country.

5. Out of respect for our flag, we must never let it touch the ground. It must be folded carefully when it is taken from the flagpole.

6. Ask the children what their state flag looks like. Tell them it is a symbol of their state and the

people who have worked hard to make it a good state.

7. Factories, schools, government buildings (such as the courthouse and post office) display flags in front of, or on top of, the buildings every day.

8. When a very important person of our country dies, flags are flown only halfway up the flagpole ("half mast") in honor of that person.

9. Get a children's book about our first flag, such as The American Flag by Ann Armbuster or Our Flag by Eleanor Ayer, and read it to the children.

10. With the children, count the stars on our flag. Each one stands for a state in the United States. Count the thirteen red and white stripes. They stand for the first thirteen colonies in our country.

11. Take a walk to look at the flag in front of, or on top of, your school, if your school displays one.

12. Let the children make flags from other countries and share them with the class.

AUGUST

PICNIC AT THE LAKE

MATERIALS AND SUPPLIES

- light blue background
- black letters
- blue and green paper
  (or newspapers or grocery bags)
- white or manila paper
- thin dinner-sized paper plate
- crayons

- scissors
- glue
- blue and green tempera paints
  (optional)
- cloth or wallpaper (optional)
- broad-tipped black marker
- Scotch Magic™ Tape

INSTRUCTIONS

1. Talk about vacations, picnics, lakes, and woods.

2. Prepare the figures from the patterns on pages 110, 113, and 115–119, using manila, white, or brown paper. Color heavily.

3. Prepare the trees from the patterns on pages 94, 131, and 140, using green and black paper. Glue the parts of the trees together.

4. Prepare the jug, ice chest, and sandwiches from the patterns on pages 177, 126, and 184, respectively. Color heavily. Prepare the sailboat from page 184.

5. Prepare the table and tablecloth from the patterns on pages 135, and 145, respectively. Color heavily.

6. Prepare the cloud from the pattern on page 172, using white paper.

7. Make the sun from the pattern on page 154.

8. Make the grass and water from green and blue paper (or from newspapers or grocery bags painted green and blue), respectively. The sizes of the grass and water are optional.

9. Outline all the shapes in black marker.

10. Tape the display to the wall.

AUGUST

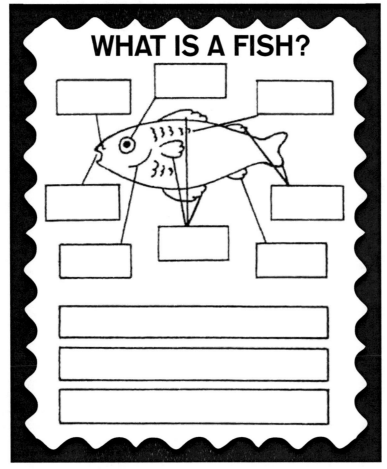

WHAT IS A FISH?

MATERIALS AND SUPPLIES

- medium blue background
- dark blue border and letters
- white paper
- crayons
- scissors
- white yarn
- wide-tipped dark blue marker
- Scotch Magic™ tape
- clear plastic

INSTRUCTIONS

1. Read about and discuss fish.

2. Prepare the fish from the pattern on page 184, using white paper. Color the fish's body orange. Use a blue marker to outline the fish and make its eye, nostril, gill cover, fins, and scales.

3. Make eight 3" by 7" labels from white paper. Use a blue marker to outline each label and to print the words: nostril, eye, scales, mouth, fin, fins (2), and gill cover.

4. Connect labels and fish art with white yarns.

5. Make three 4" by 14" labels from white paper. Use a blue marker to outline each label and to print these facts: Fish have backbones. They live in the water. Fish provide us with food.

6. To give the entire bulletin board an underwater effect, cover it with clear plastic.

AUGUST

WHAT IS A FAIR?

MATERIALS AND SUPPLIES

- dark brown cloth background
- white border
- white letters

- crayons
- scissors

- any white paper that crayons can write on (Used computer paper, clean on one side, is OK.)

From *Big Book of Bulletin Boards for Every Month*. Copyright © 2006 Good Year Books.

INSTRUCTIONS

1. From the pattern on page 185, make a Ferris wheel. Color and cut it out around the outer edges.

2. Using the patterns, color and cut out: pig, cow, and chicken, p. 165; sheep, p. 166; lamp and bread, p. 99; cheese, p. 168; jacket, p. 101; carrot, p. 148; pumpkin, p. 159 or p. 137; potato, p. 144.

3. Discuss fairs with the children. Ask the children if they have been to one. Ask what things they saw and what they liked best. Write these things on the chalkboard: rides,

exhibits (ribbons awarded), games, animals (ribbons awarded), races, food, vegetable and fruit displays, clothing and cake displays, advertisements, farm equipment, tractor pulls, and so on.

4. Ask the children to write about the fair and draw pictures of the things they like best.

5. Children whose families have exhibited animals can tell and write about their experiences.

6. Display the children's stories and art work beyond the bulletin board.

PROJECT PATTERNS

Tree Trunk, Crown

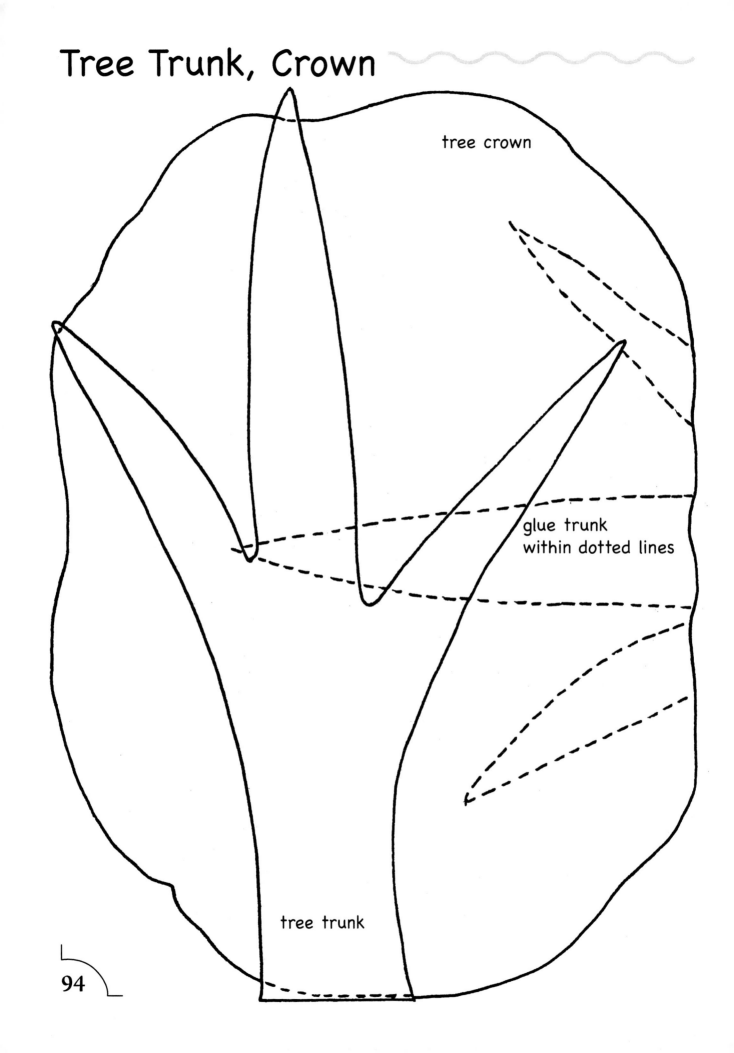

tree crown

glue trunk
within dotted lines

tree trunk

Cupcake,
Sun,

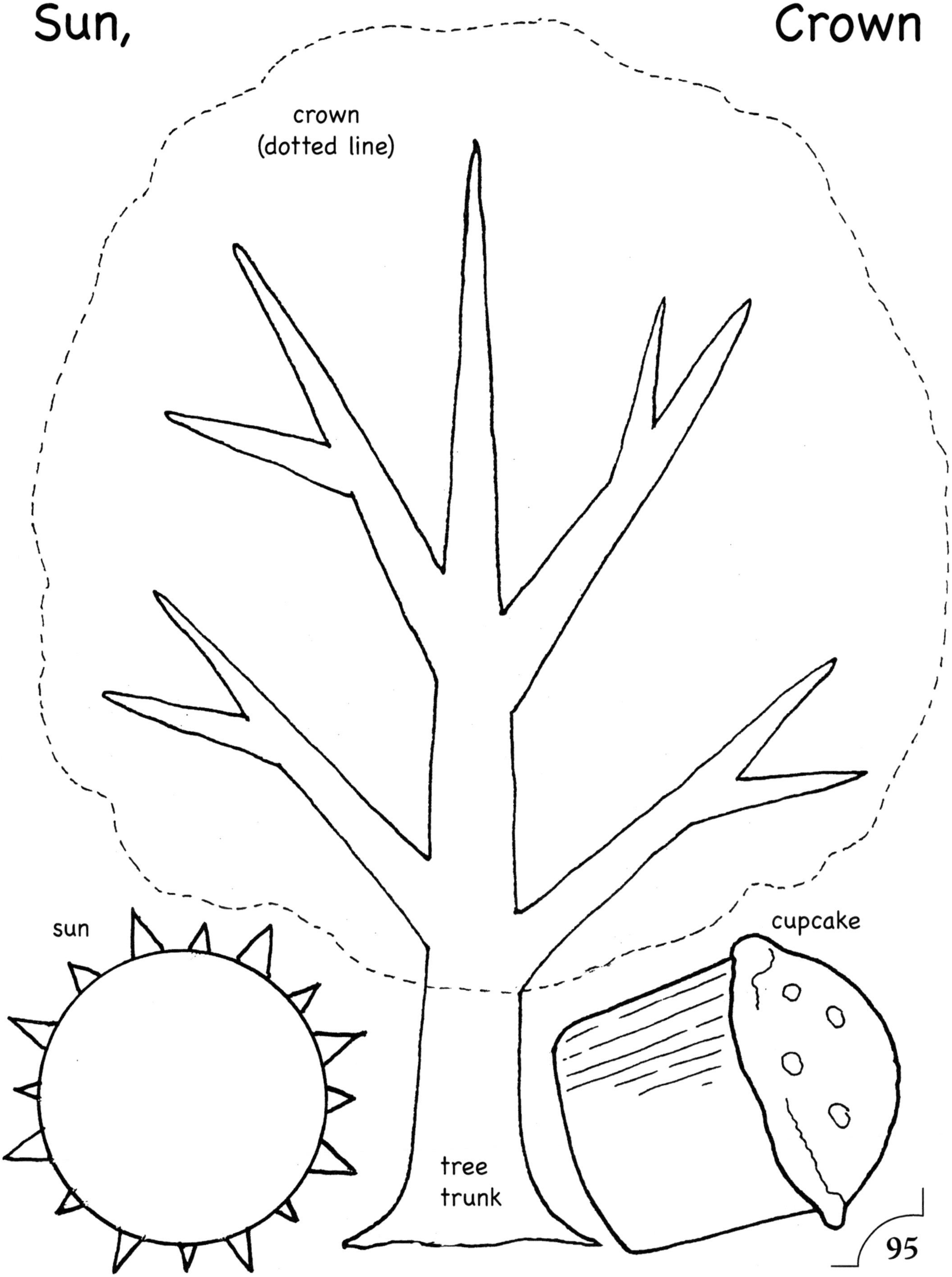

crown
(dotted line)

sun

cupcake

tree
trunk

95

Strawberry,
Hands,
Boy,
Chicks,
Staff

walking staff

boy

chicks

strawberry

Boy, Cap, Turnip, Moon, Kitten

kitten

moon

boy

turnip

cap

Tree Trunk,
Snake,
Girl

tree
trunk

girl

snake

98

Girl,
Bread,
Ham,
Lamp

girl

ham

bread

lamp

Girl, Button
Mouth,
Bud 3,
Root

girl

bud 3

button
mouth

root

From *Big Book of Bulletin Boards for Every Month*. Copyright © 2006 Good Year Books.

Boy, Apple,
Jacket,
Boots

apple

boy

boots

jacket

101

Face, Duck

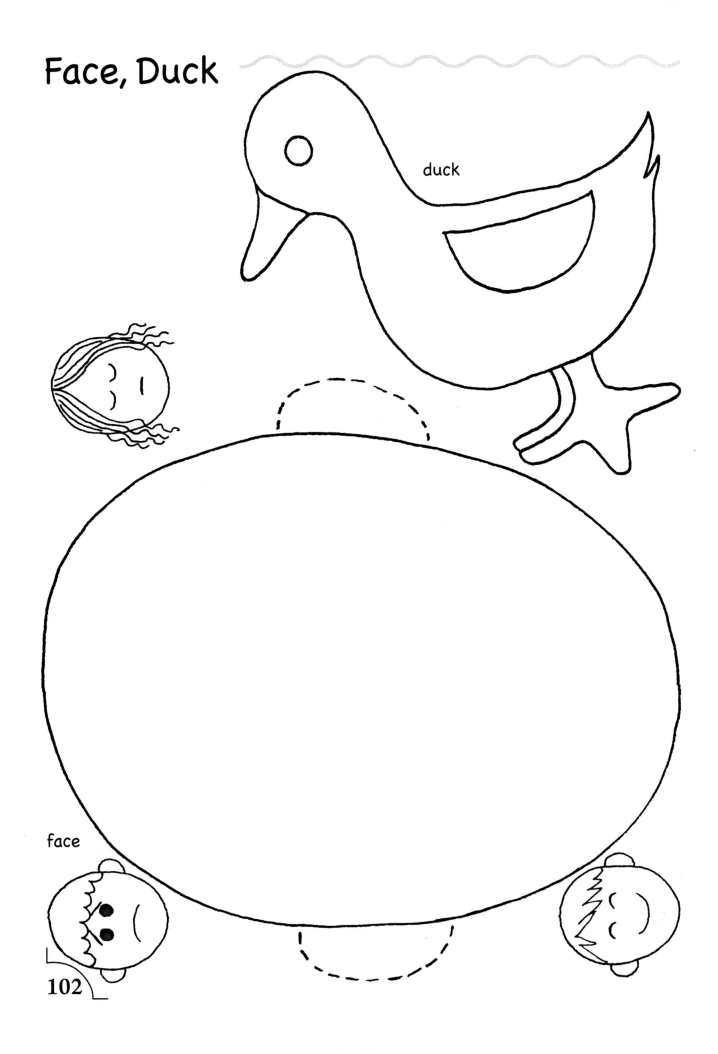

duck

face

Boy/Girl Face, Arm, Eyes

boy face
(girl face—
dotted line)

arm

eyes

Boy/Girl Bottom, Arm,
Rainforest Leaf, Banana Leaf

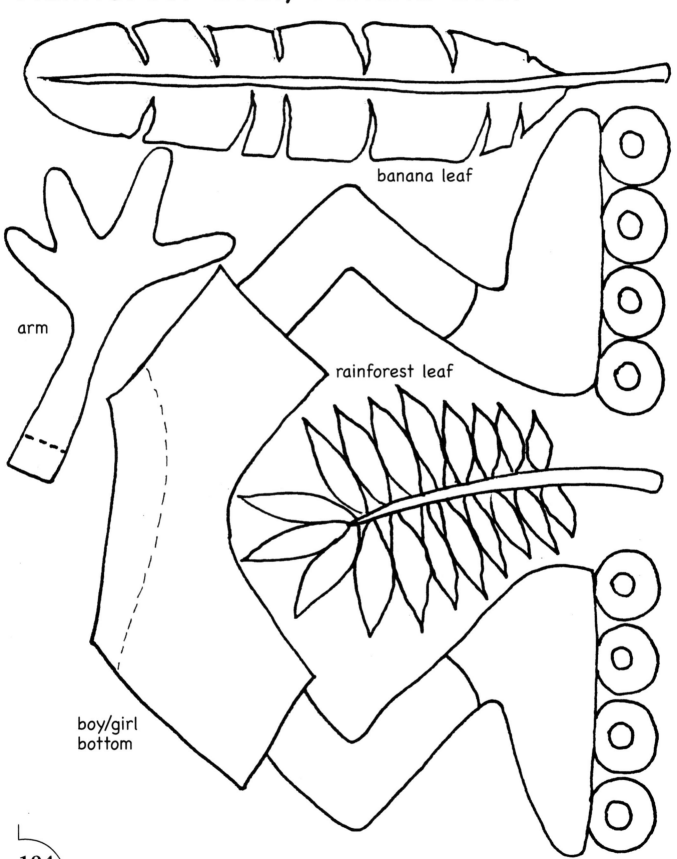

banana leaf

arm

rainforest leaf

boy/girl
bottom

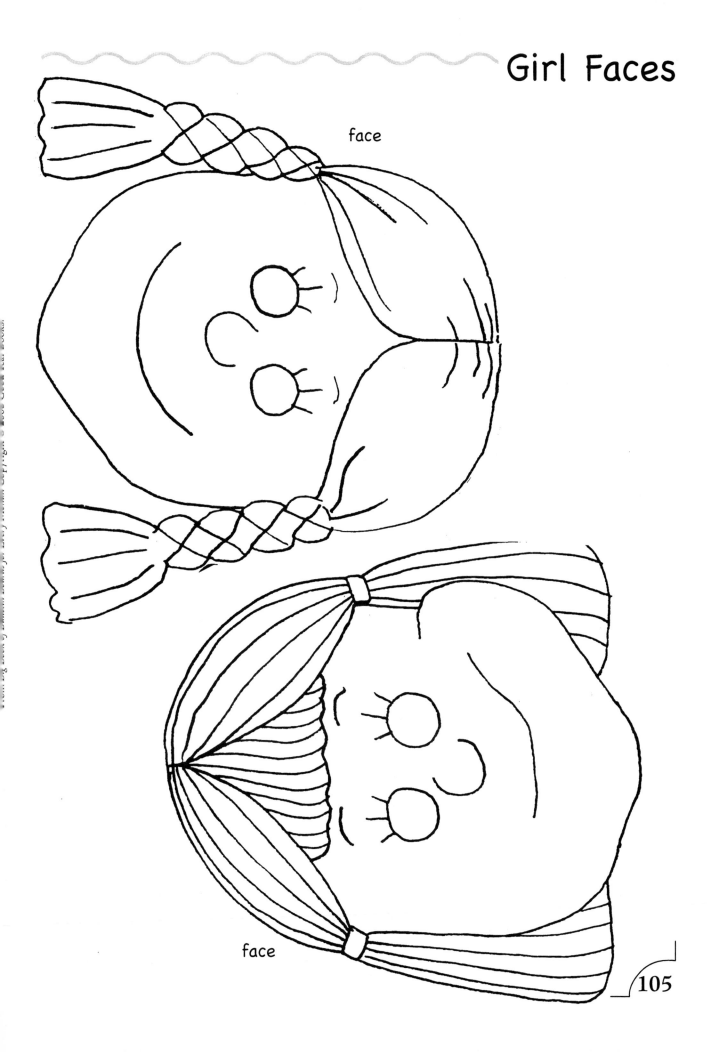

face

face

Sad or Angry Mouth, Faces, Missing Teeth, Angry Eyebrows, Tongues

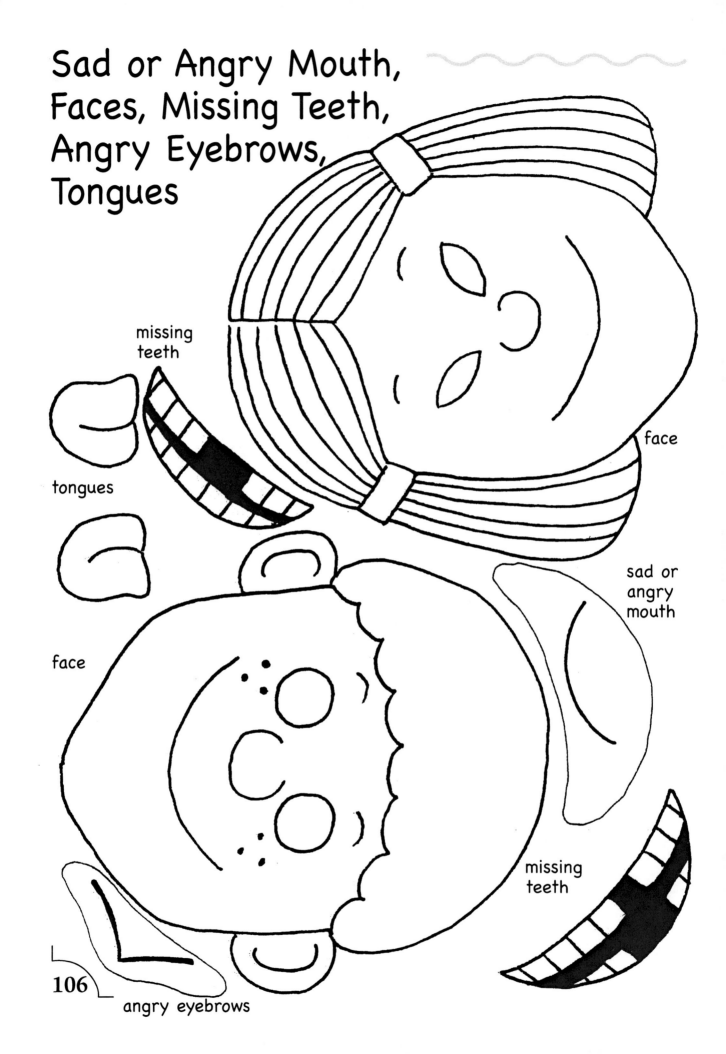

missing teeth

tongues

face

face

sad or angry mouth

missing teeth

angry eyebrows

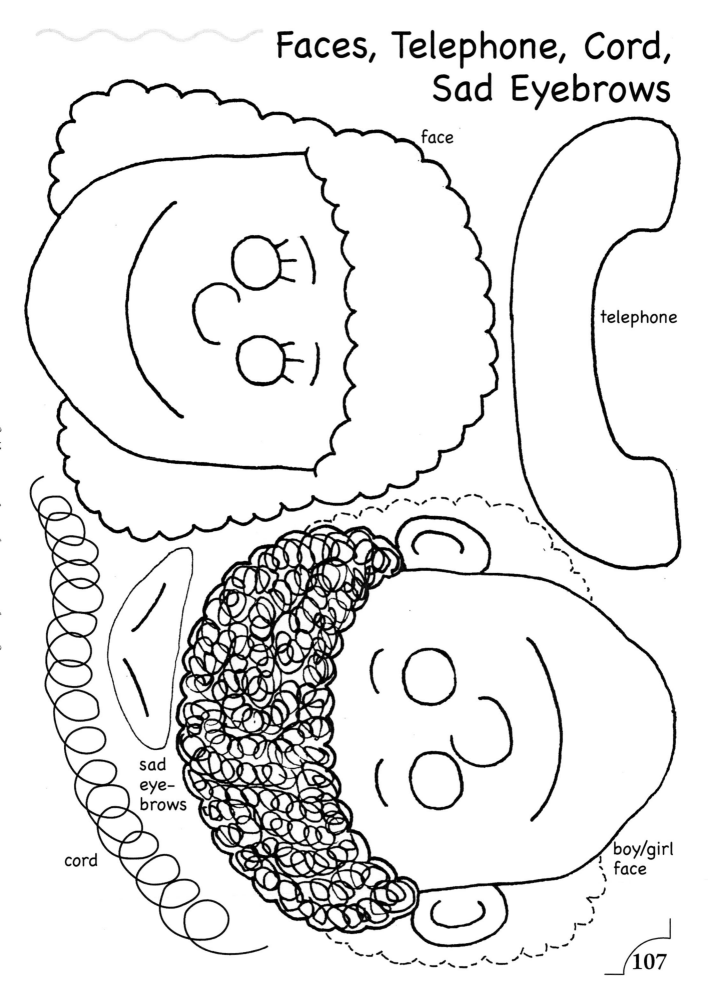

Faces, Telephone, Cord,
Sad Eyebrows

face

telephone

sad eye-brows

cord

boy/girl face

Danny Dibby,
Leg, Arm, Ear

Danny Dibby

leg

arm

ear

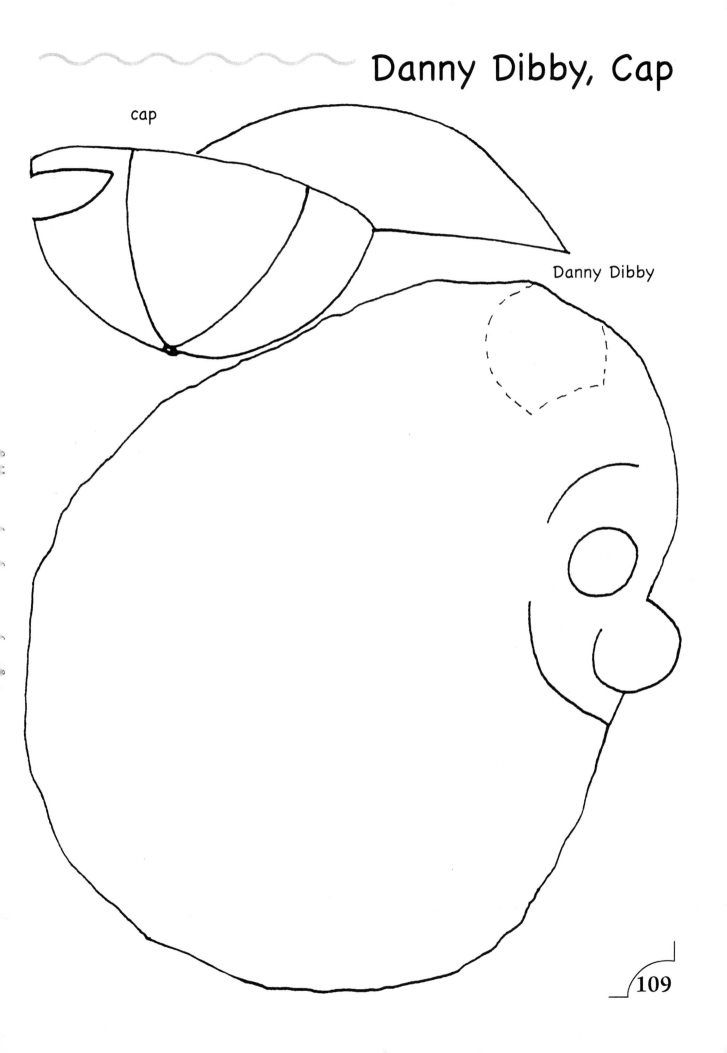

Danny Dibby, Cap

cap

Danny Dibby

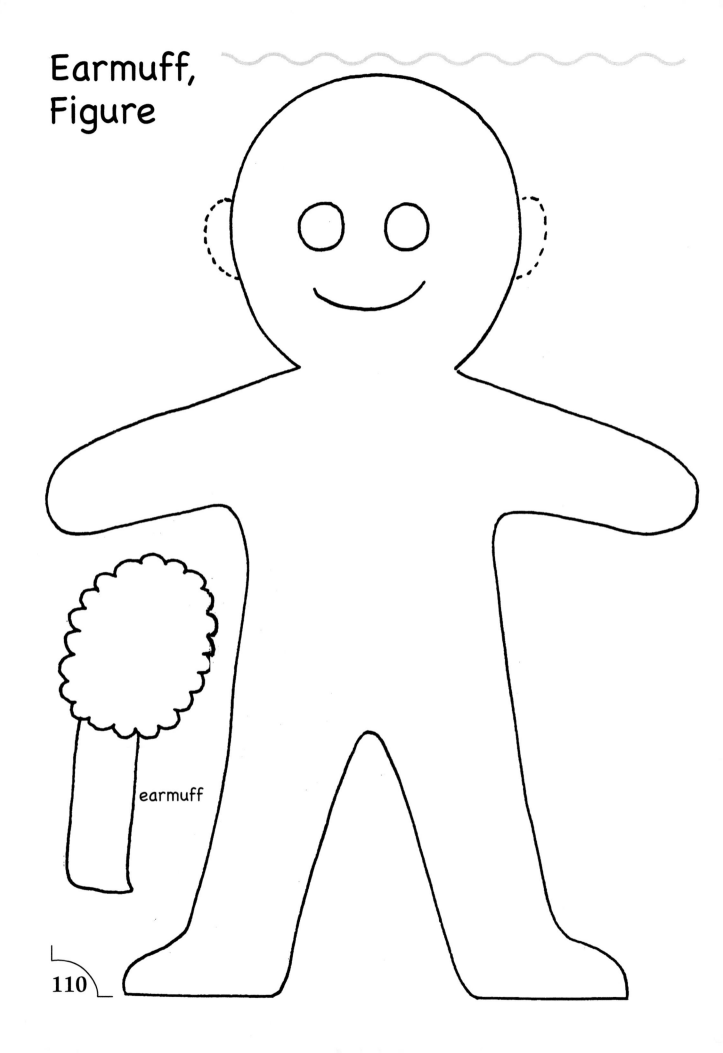

Earmuff,
Figure

earmuff

110

Cats A and B

cat A

cat B

Cats C and D

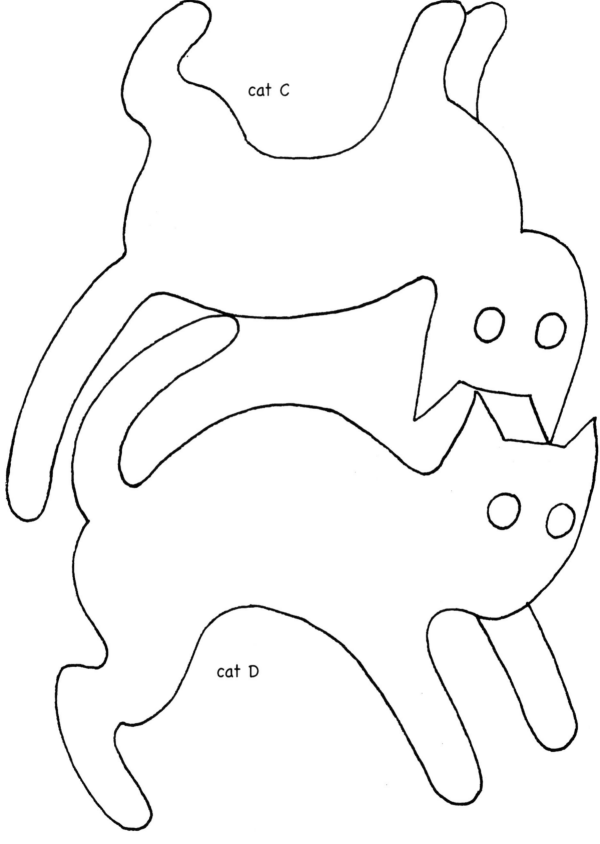

cat C

cat D

From *Big Book of Bulletin Boards for Every Month*. Copyright © 2006 Good Year Books.

Flower, Figure

line for
boy, running

flower

Traffic Light, Waves

traffic light

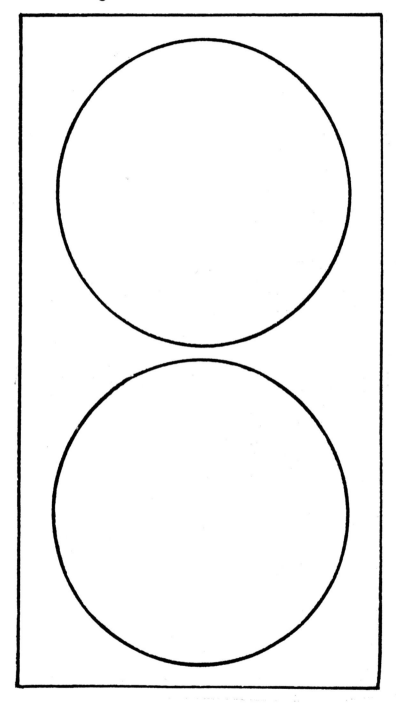

waves

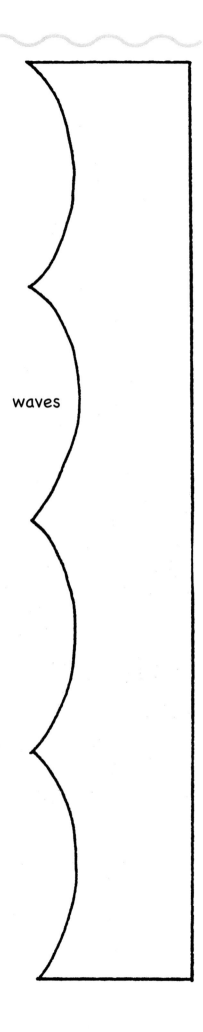

Figures,
Trash
Can

trash can

115

Figures,
Tooth,
Drum

tooth

drum

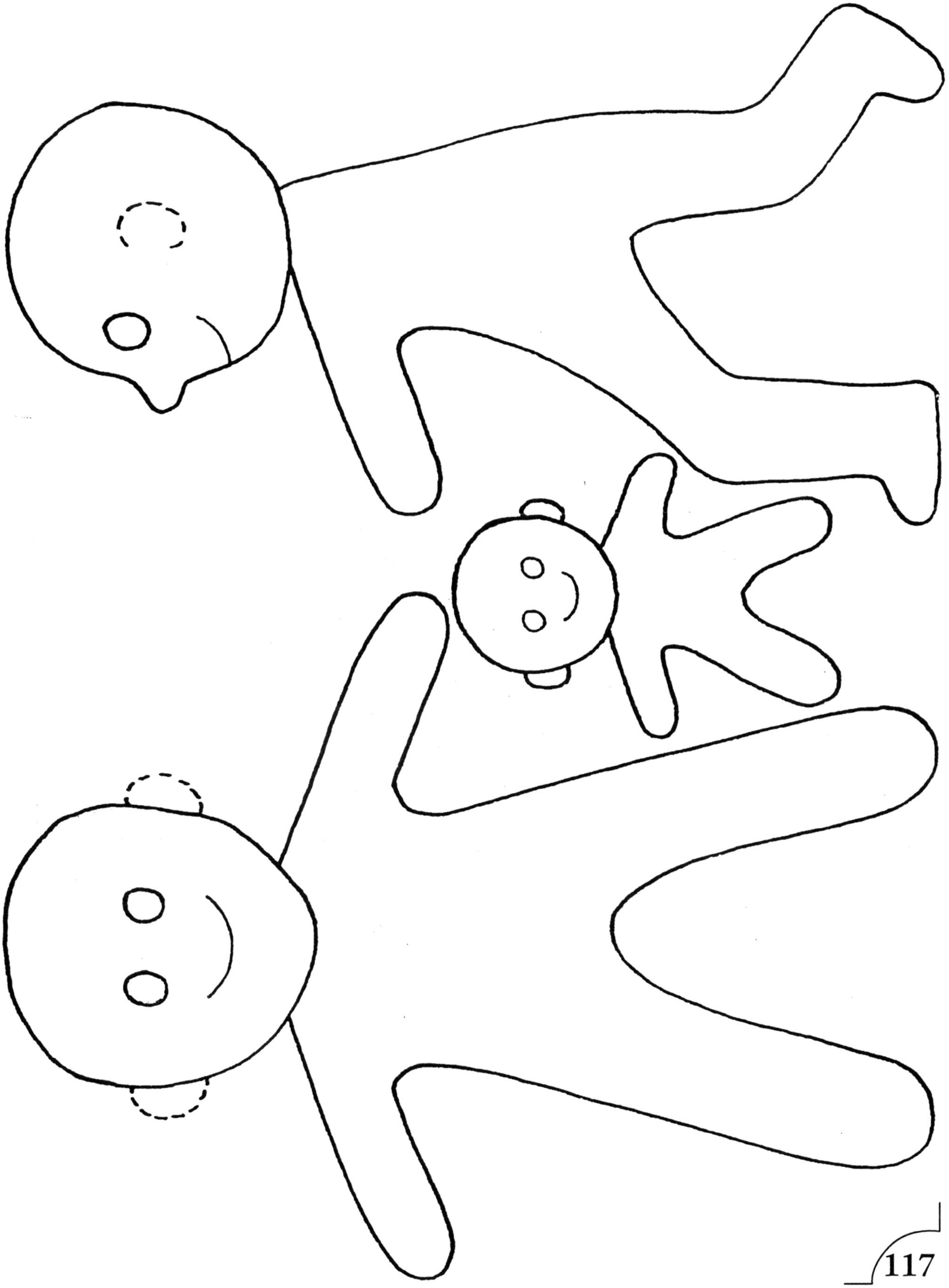

Basketball, Hoop,
Figures, Doll, Skateboard

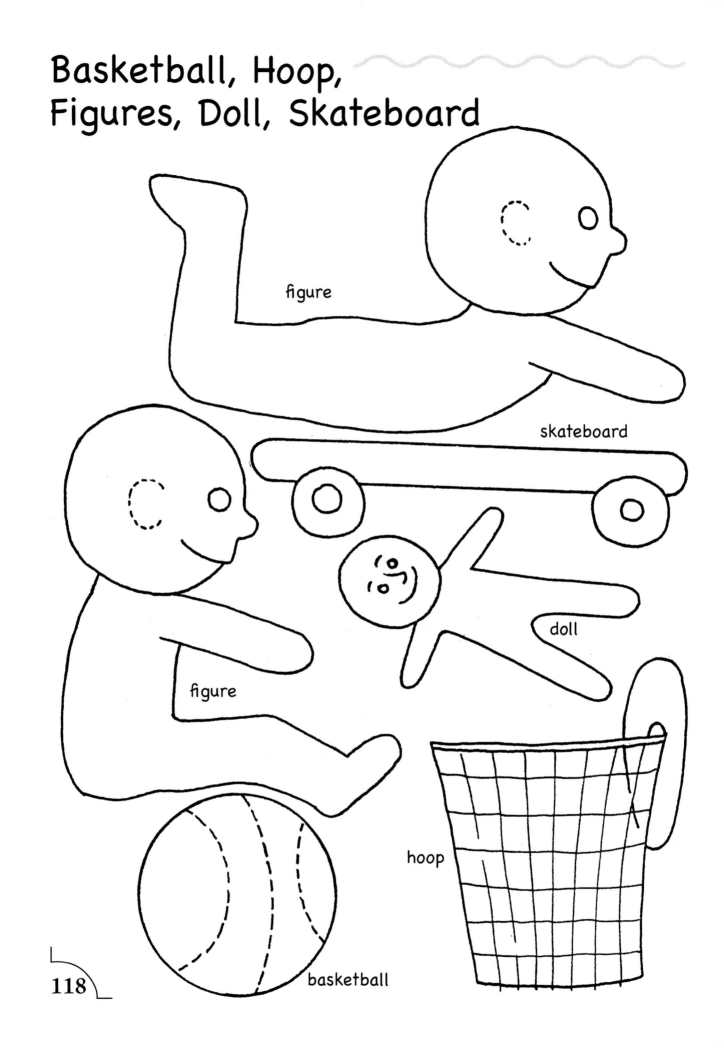

figure

skateboard

figure

doll

hoop

basketball

figure

girl

road

figure

Mayflower

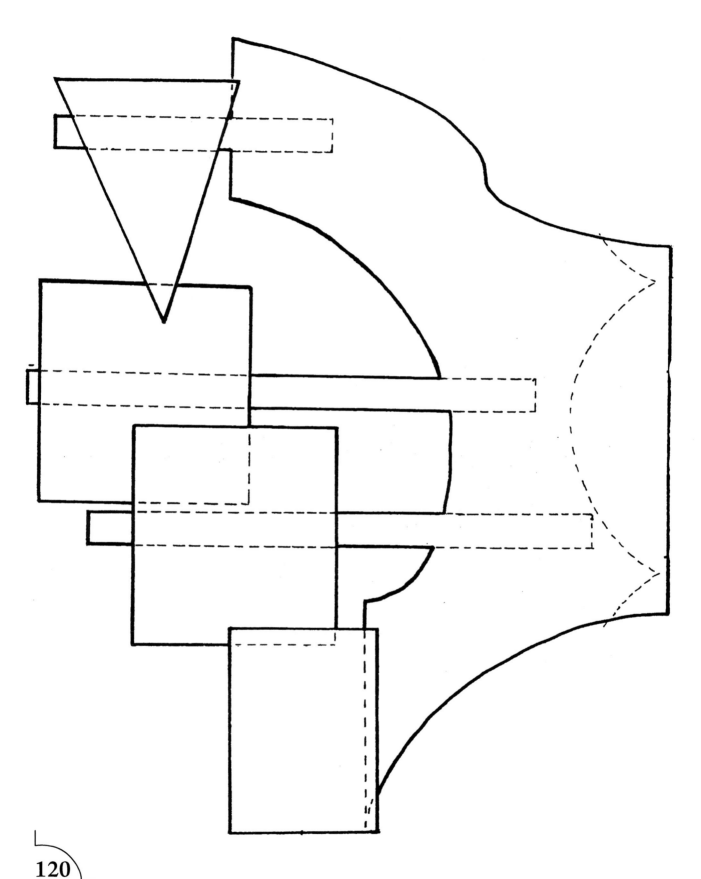

Leaves—Oak, Green, Poplar, Maple, Cottonwood

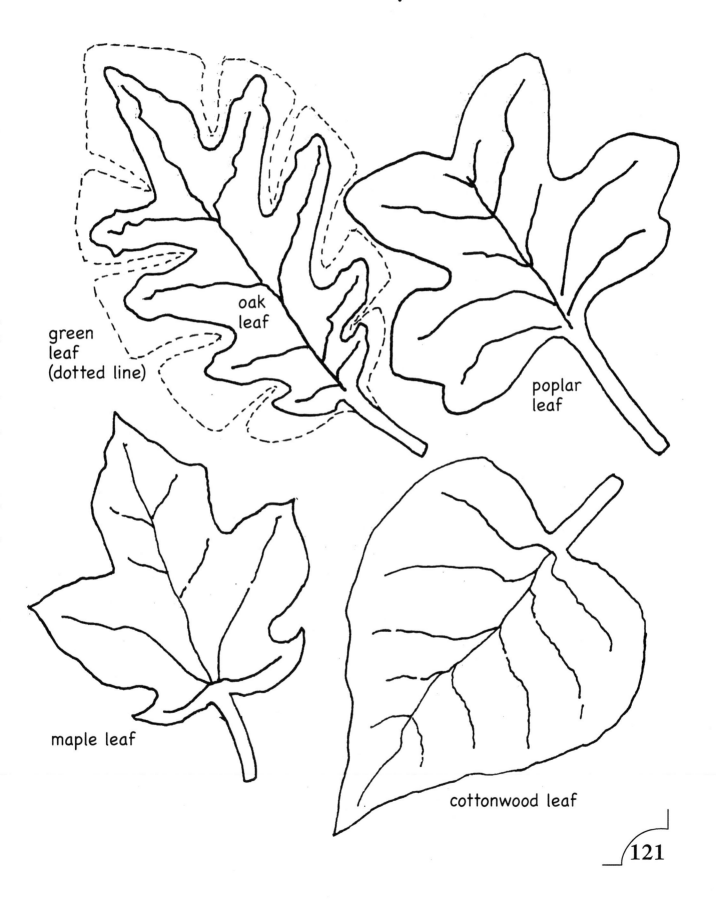

green
leaf
(dotted line)

oak
leaf

poplar
leaf

maple leaf

cottonwood leaf

Body, Shoes, Legs

left leg

right leg

left shoe

right shoe

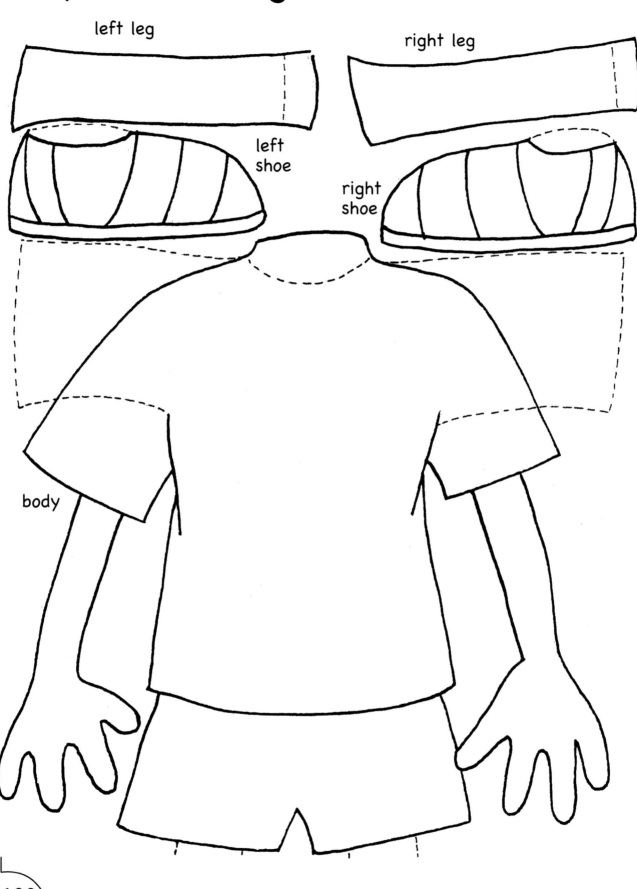

body

Ship,
Bottom

ship (bottom)

123

Ship,
Top

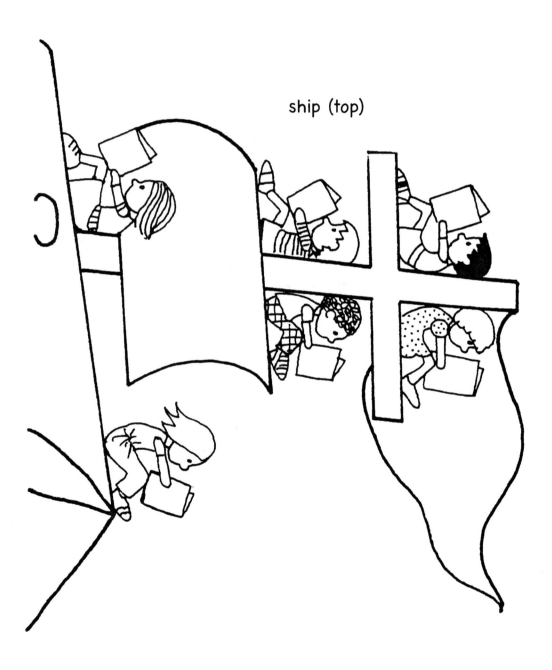

ship (top)

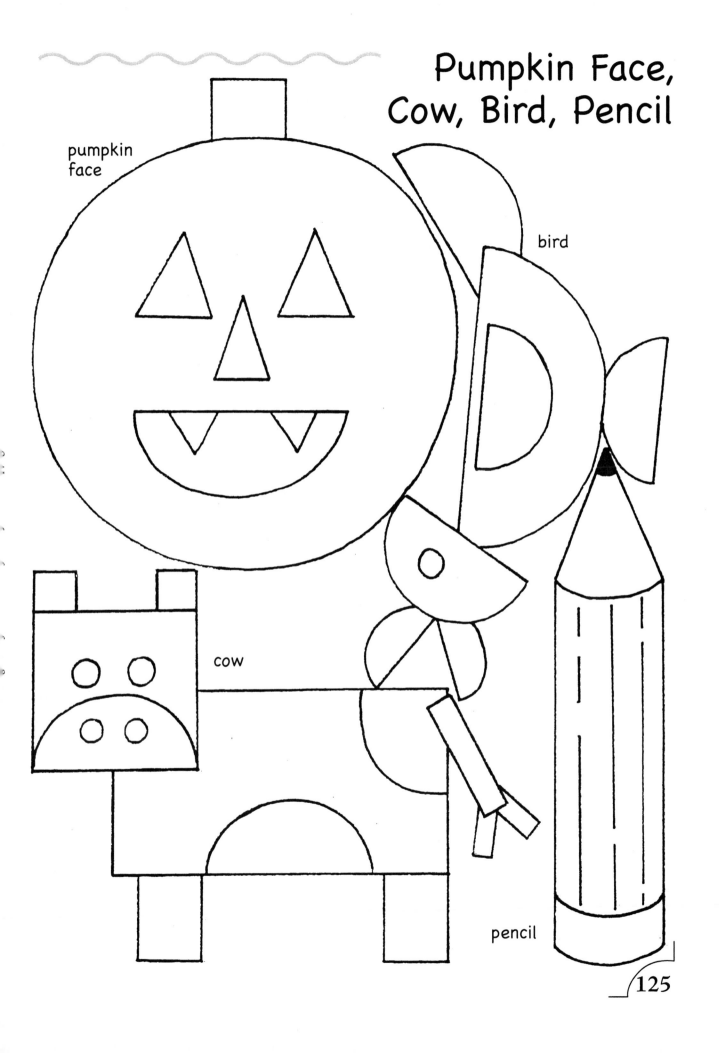

Pumpkin Face, Cow, Bird, Pencil

pumpkin
face

bird

cow

pencil

125

Ice Chest, Robot, Car, Spider Monkey, Monkey's Tail

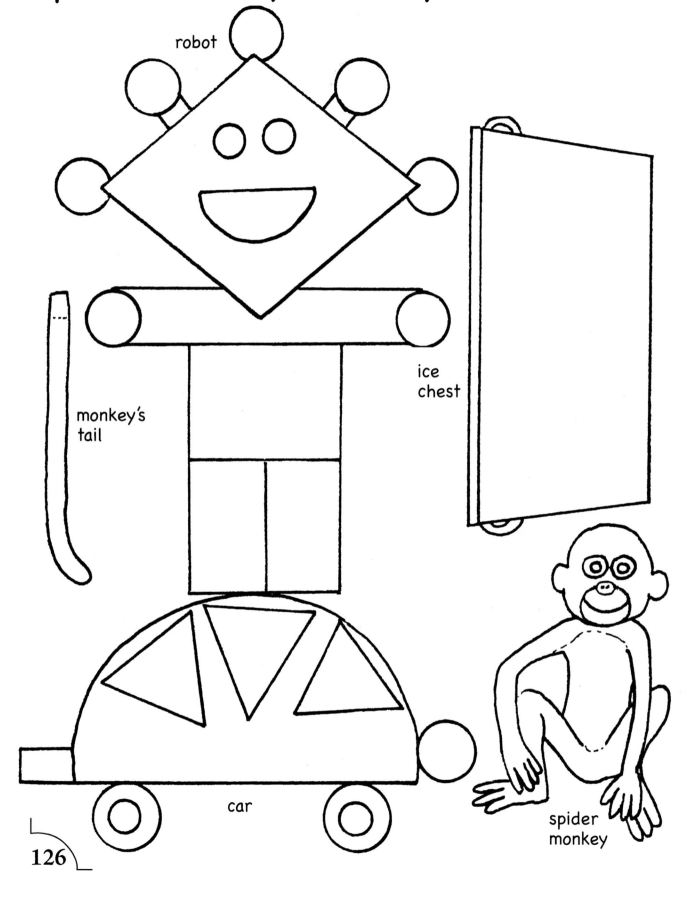

robot

ice chest

monkey's tail

car

spider monkey

126

Voting Booths, Witch

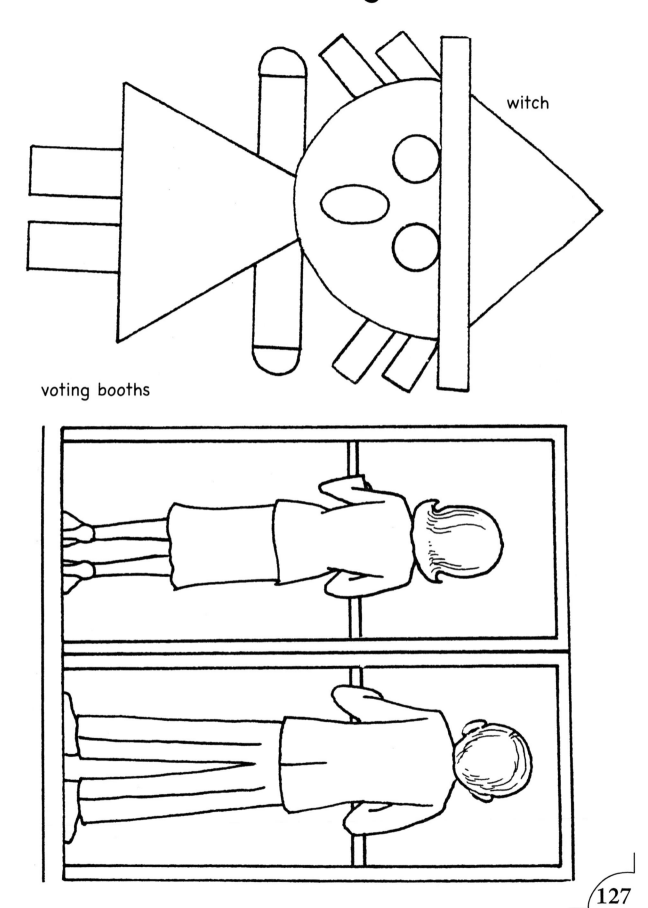

witch

voting booths

Orange-tree Crown, Raccoon, Nuts, Corn, Orange, Sunflower Seed

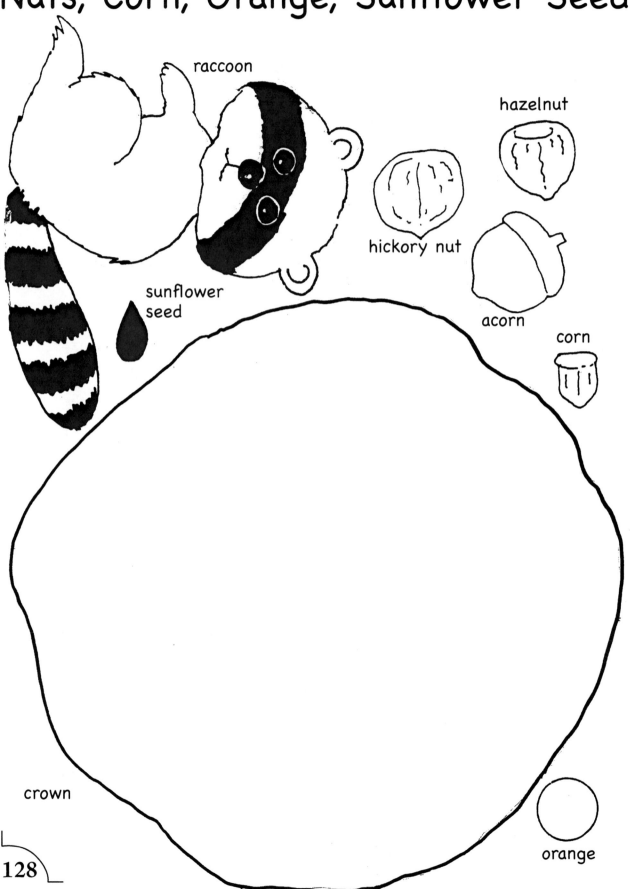

raccoon

hazelnut

hickory nut

acorn

corn

sunflower seed

crown

orange

Big Ghost,
Leaves

little
leaf

big
leaf

big ghost

129

Pilgrim House, Roasted Turkey, Bowl

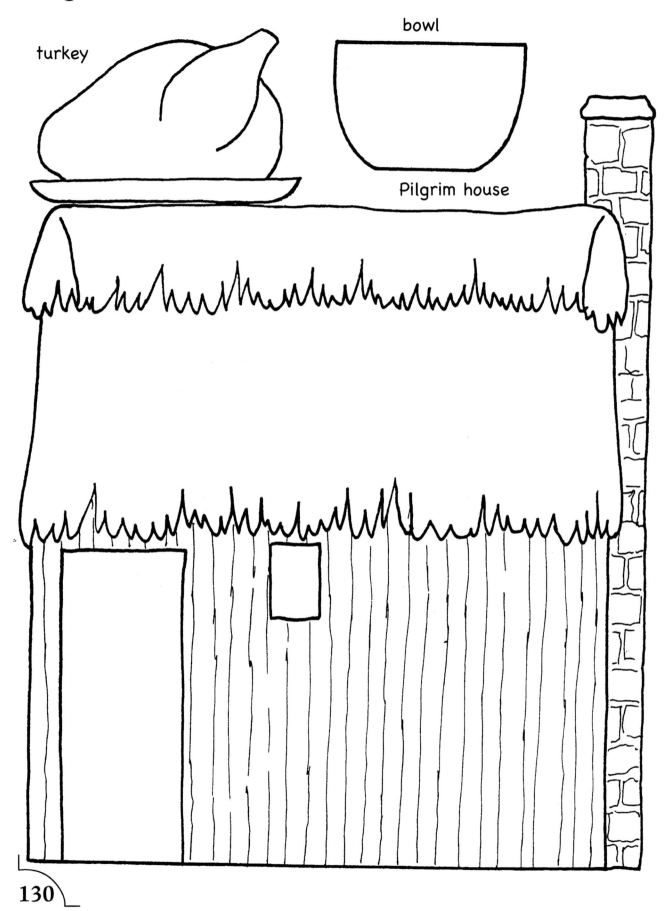

turkey

bowl

Pilgrim house

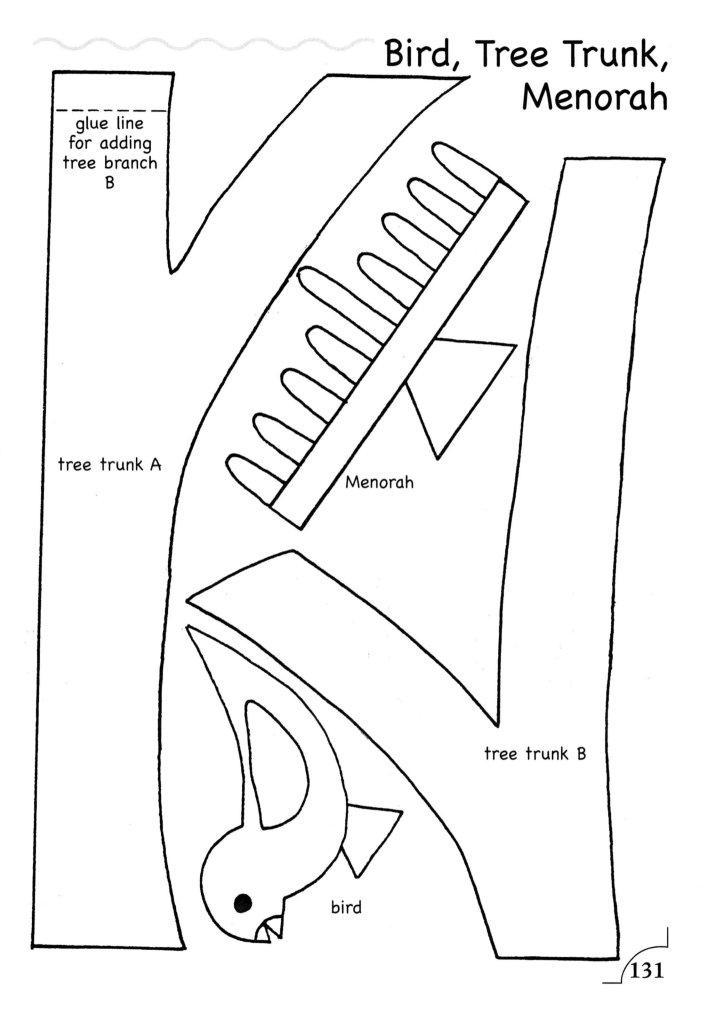

Bird, Tree Trunk, Menorah

glue line
for adding
tree branch
B

tree trunk A

Menorah

tree trunk B

bird

Winter
Tree Trunk,
Smaller Tree
Trunk,
Crown

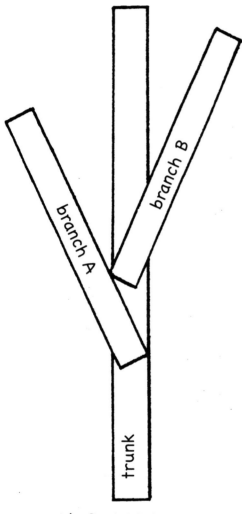

branch B

branch A

trunk

5 ¹/₂ feet high
3 foot branches

Cut a 36"
square or 24"
or 12" square

crown

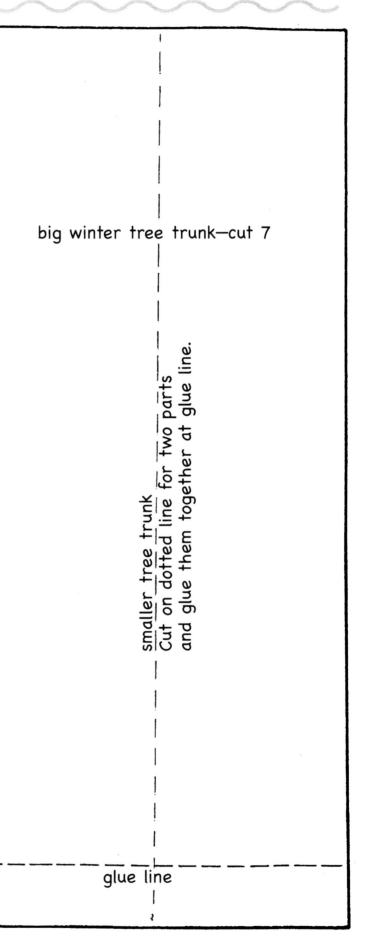

big winter tree trunk—cut 7

smaller tree trunk
Cut on dotted line for two parts
and glue them together at glue line.

glue line

From *Big Book of Bulletin Boards for Every Month.* Copyright © 2006 Good Year Books.

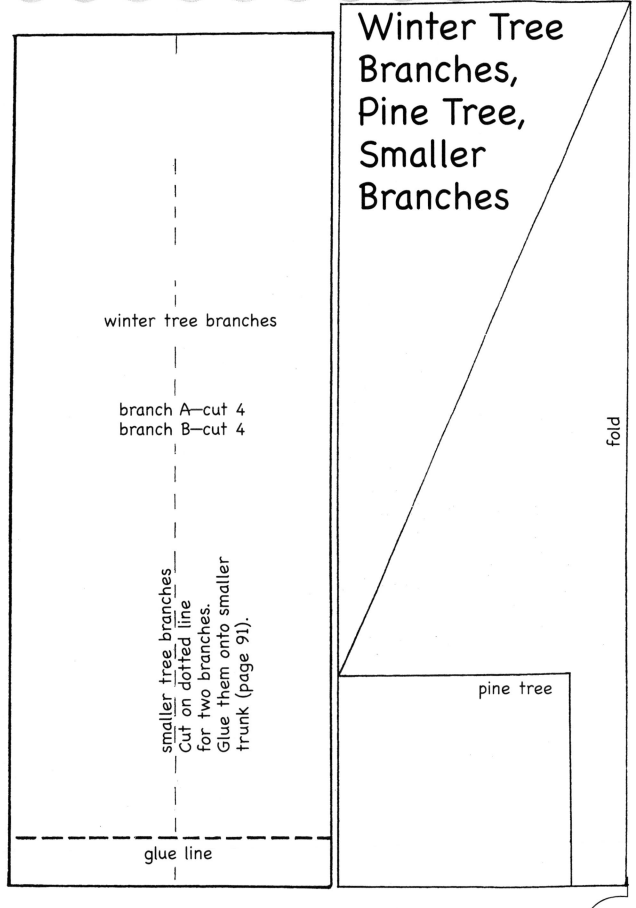

Winter Tree Branches, Pine Tree, Smaller Branches

winter tree branches

branch A—cut 4
branch B—cut 4

smaller tree branches
Cut on dotted line
for two branches.
Glue them onto smaller
trunk (page 91).

glue line

fold

pine tree

Turkey Head, Legs, Feet, Grocery Cart, Feathers

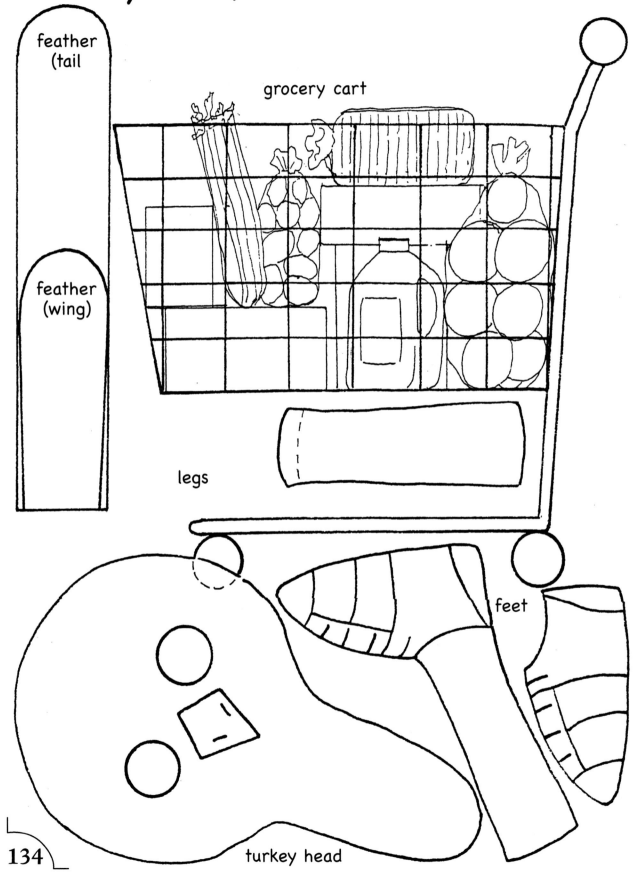

feather (tail

feather (wing)

grocery cart

legs

feet

turkey head

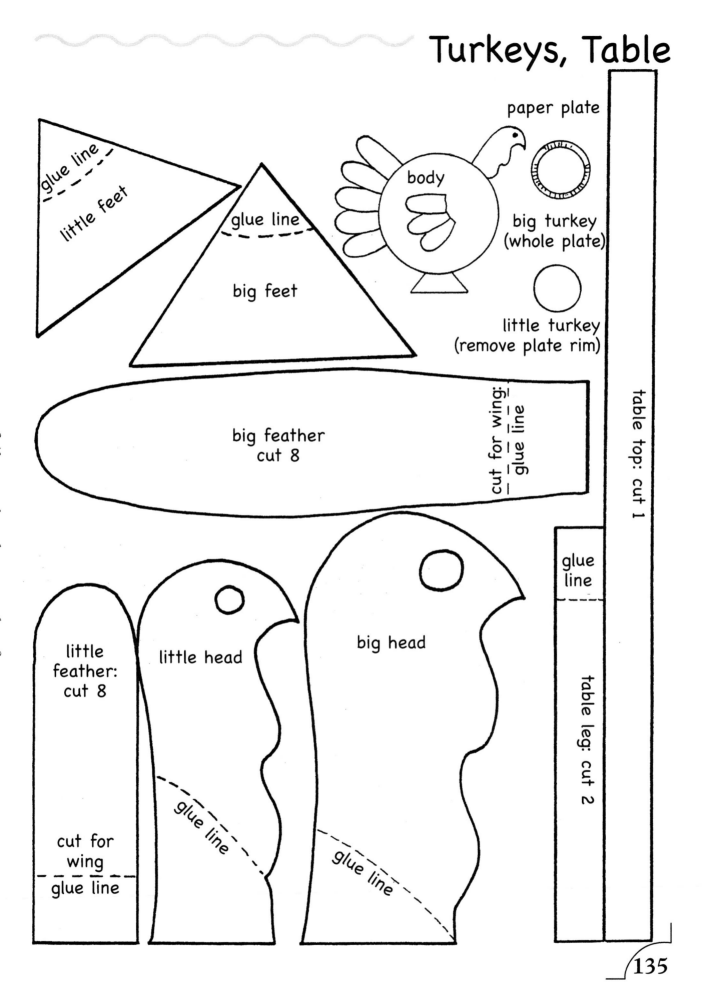

Turkeys, Table

paper plate

little feet

glue line

big feet

glue line

body

big turkey
(whole plate)

little turkey
(remove plate rim)

big feather
cut 8

cut for wing:
glue line

table top: cut 1

little
feather:
cut 8

little head

big head

glue line

table leg: cut 2

cut for
wing
glue line

glue line

glue line

Elephant, Donkey, Crayon

elephant

donkey

crayon

Pumpkin

pumpkin

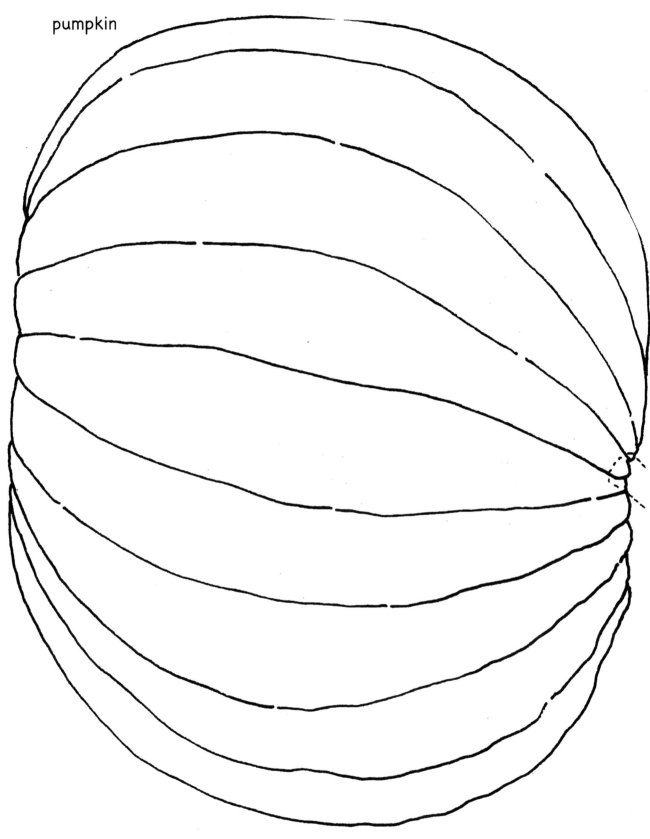

Pumpkin Vine, Flower, Duck

flower

duck

pumpkin vine

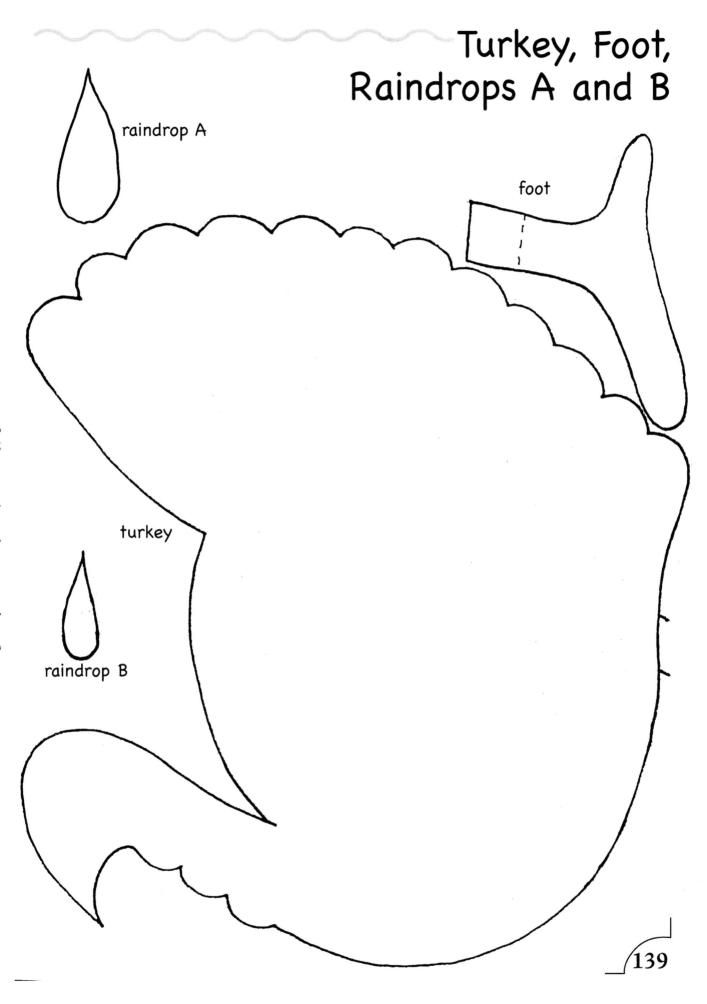

raindrop A

Turkey, Foot,
Raindrops A and B

foot

turkey

raindrop B

Big and Small Christmas Trees, Ornament, Trunk, Snowball

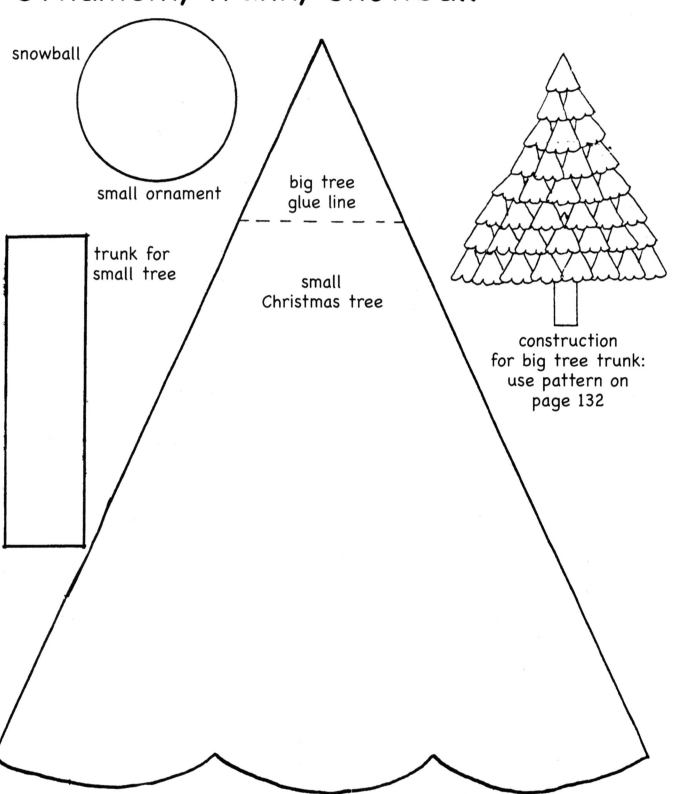

snowball

small ornament

trunk for small tree

big tree glue line

small Christmas tree

construction for big tree trunk: use pattern on page 132

Palm Tree Trunk, Stable, Star, Sheep, Manger, Baby Jesus, Shepherd's Staff

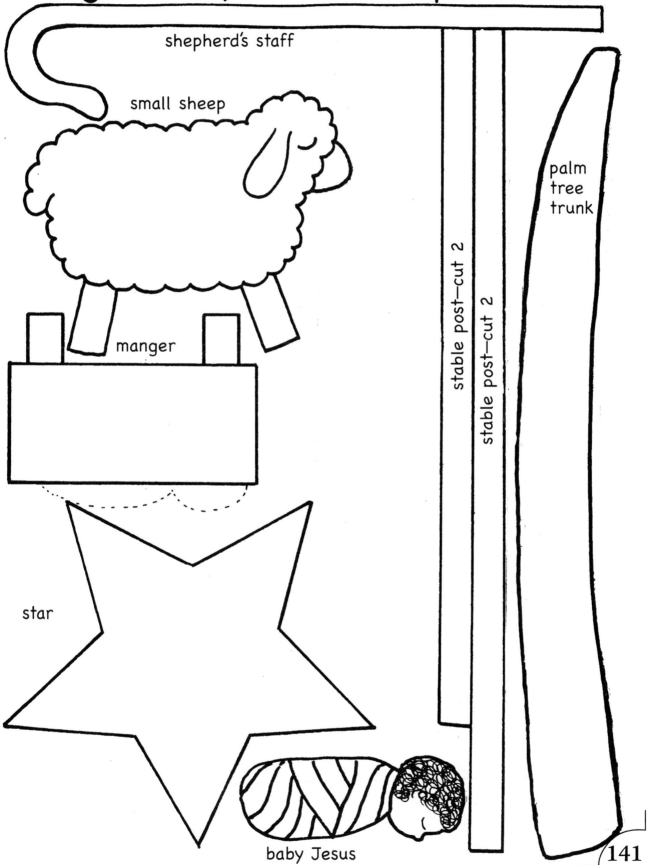

shepherd's staff

small sheep

manger

palm tree trunk

stable post—cut 2

stable post—cut 2

star

baby Jesus

Pie, Cow

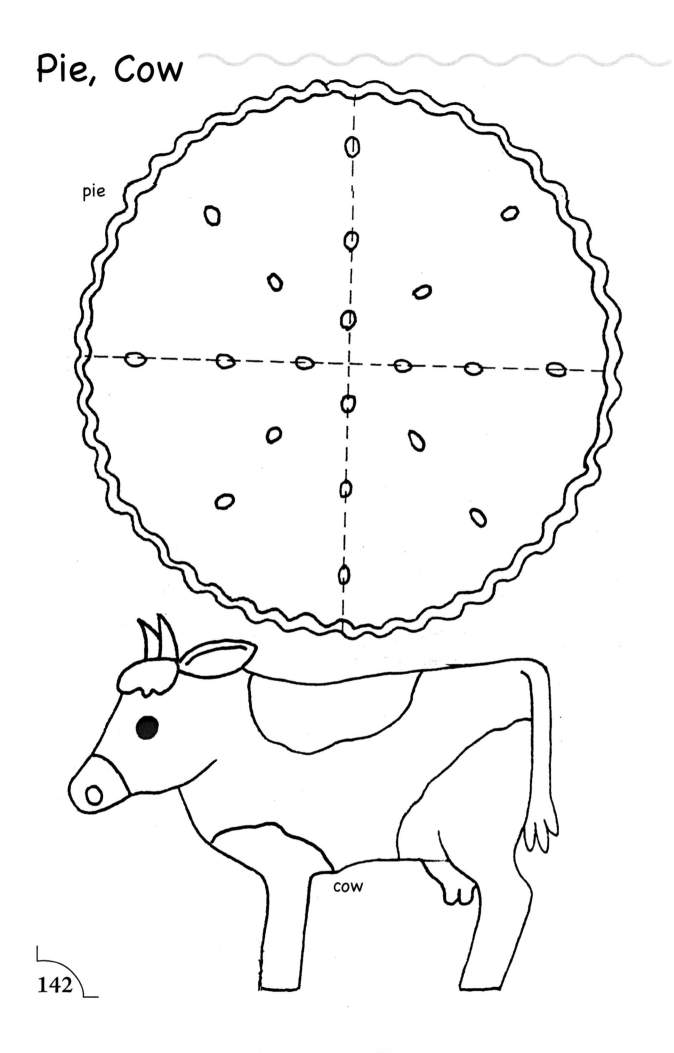

pie

cow

Desserts, Hand, Serious Mouth, Angry Eye

dessert

serious mouth

hand (mitten)

angry eye

dessert

Cantaloupe, Candle, Potato, Star

potato

star

candle

cantaloupe

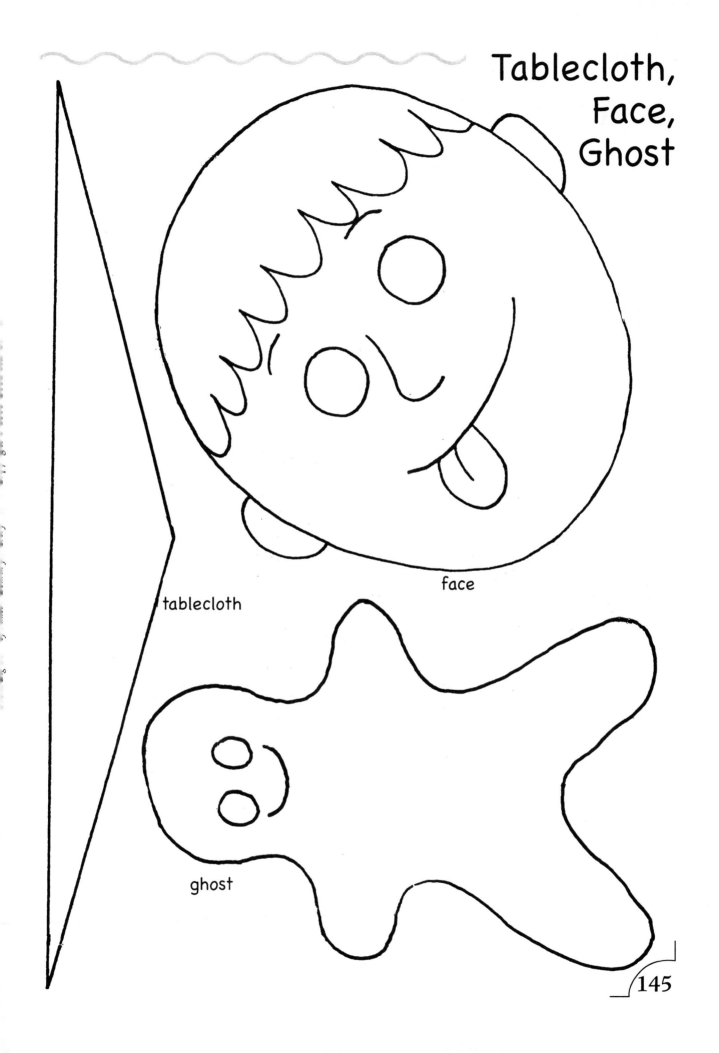

Tablecloth,
Face,
Ghost

tablecloth

face

ghost

145

Bell, Candy Cane,
Sheep, Scarf

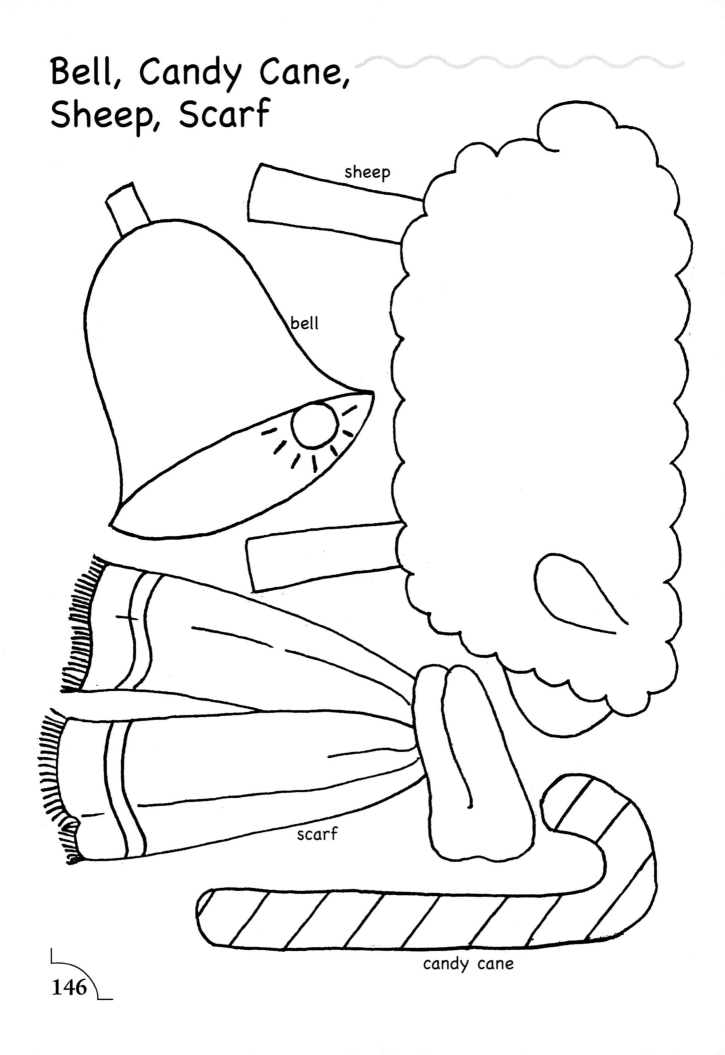

sheep

bell

scarf

candy cane

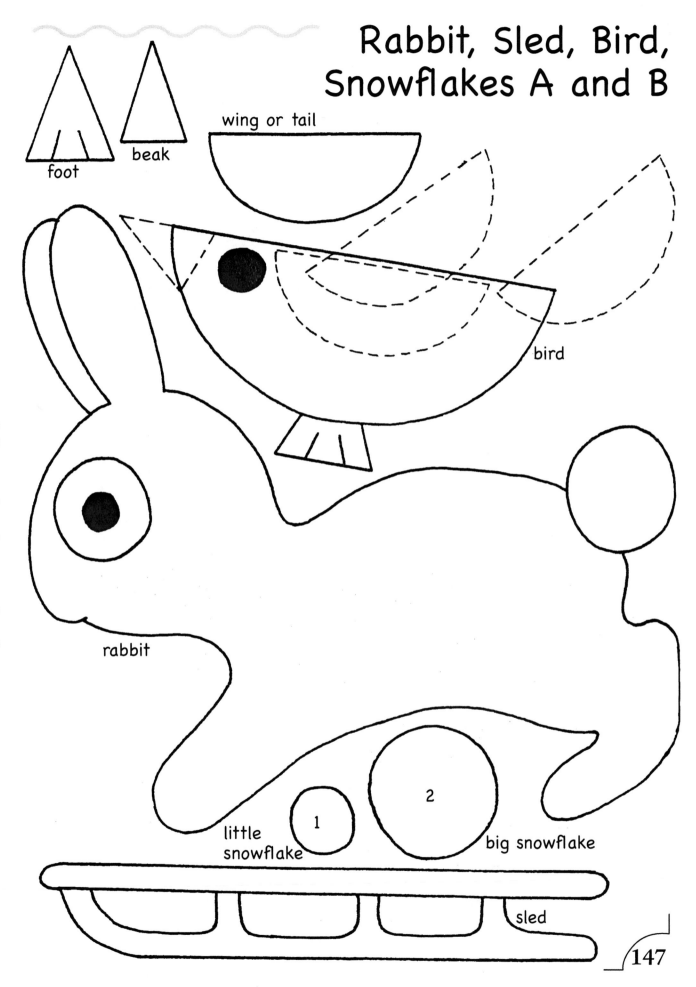

Rabbit, Sled, Bird,
Snowflakes A and B

foot

beak

wing or tail

bird

rabbit

little
snowflake

1

2

big snowflake

sled

Bird, Carrot, Hat

carrot

bird

hat

Face, Hand, Question Mark, Seed, Sprouts, Buds 1 and 2

face

question
mark

sprout 3

hand

bud 2

sprout 2

sprout 4

sprout 1

bud 1

seed

Weather Symbols, Potatoes, Hat, Rain Hat, Scarf

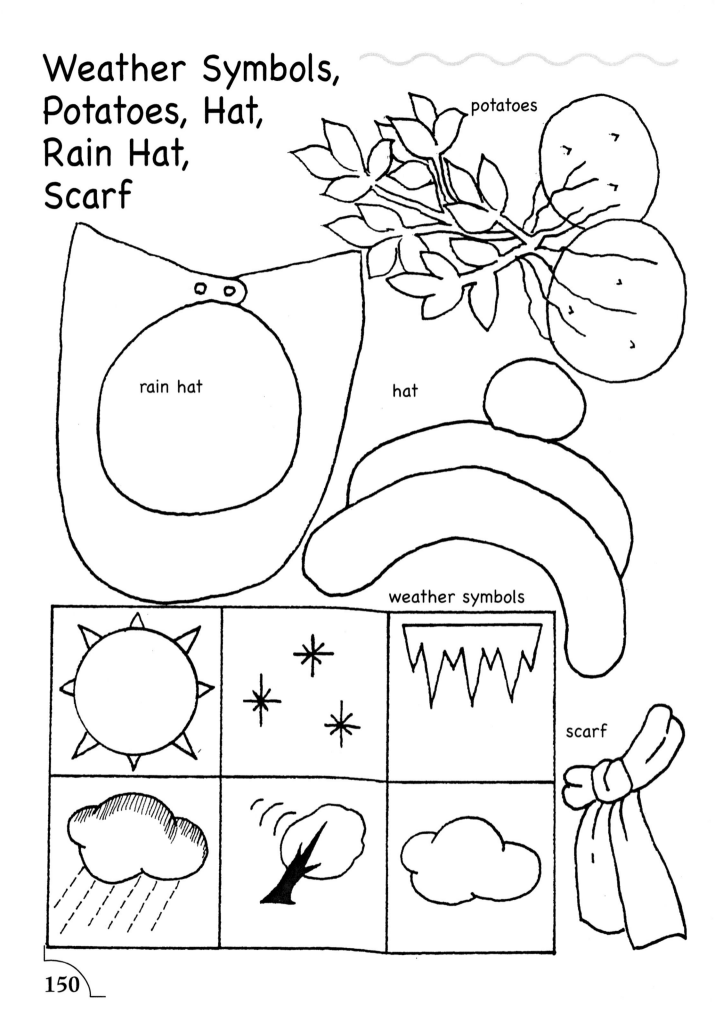

potatoes

rain hat

hat

weather symbols

scarf

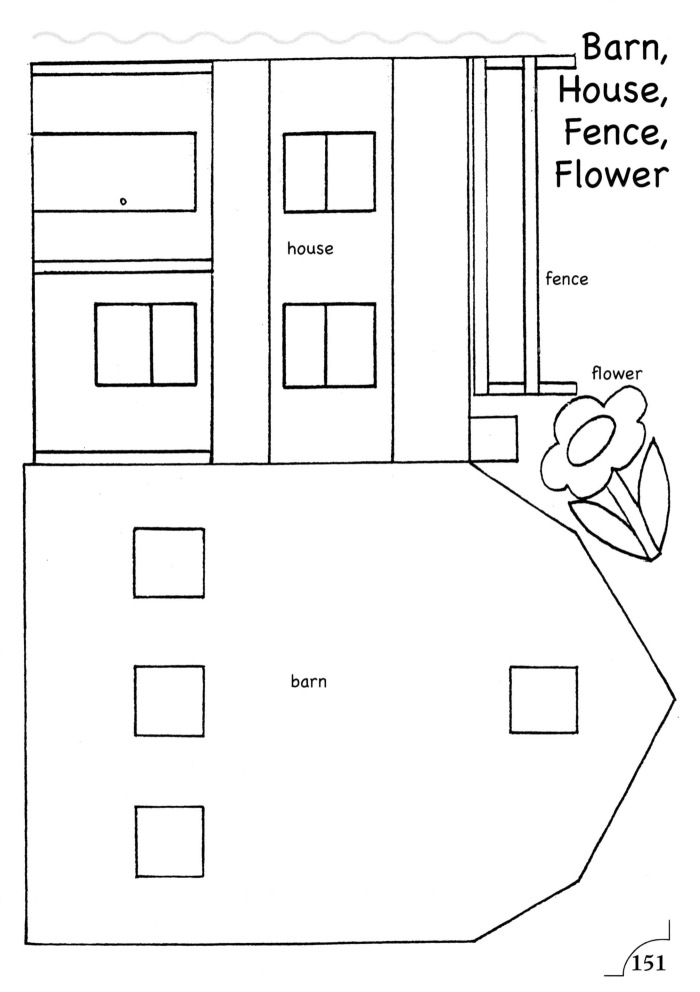

Barn,
House,
Fence,
Flower

house

fence

flower

barn

Boy, Feet, Radish, Beet

radish

boy

beet

feet

Watermelon, Pear, Lemon, Plum, Banana, Kiwi, Mango, Raspberry

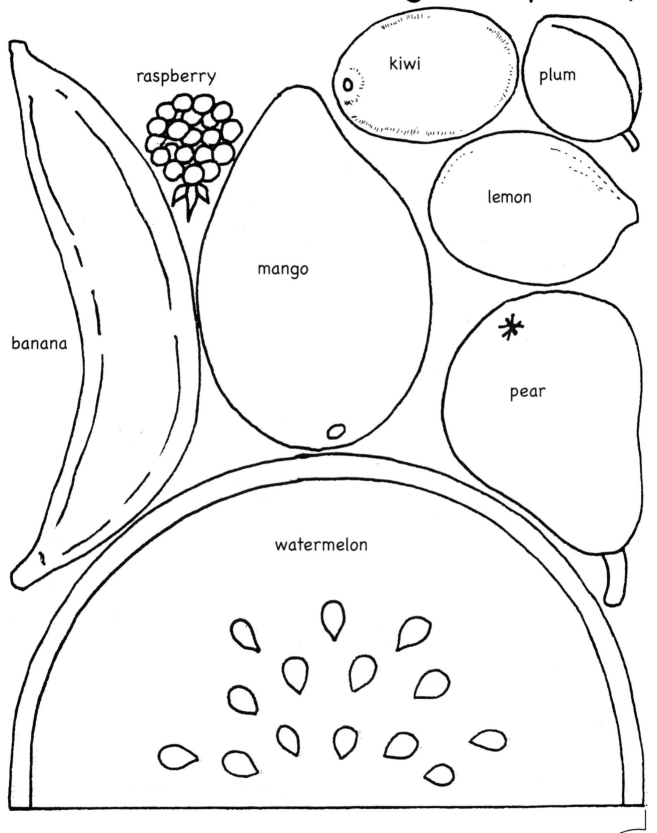

Grapes, In-line Skates A and B, Palm Leaf, Big Snowman or Ornament or Sun

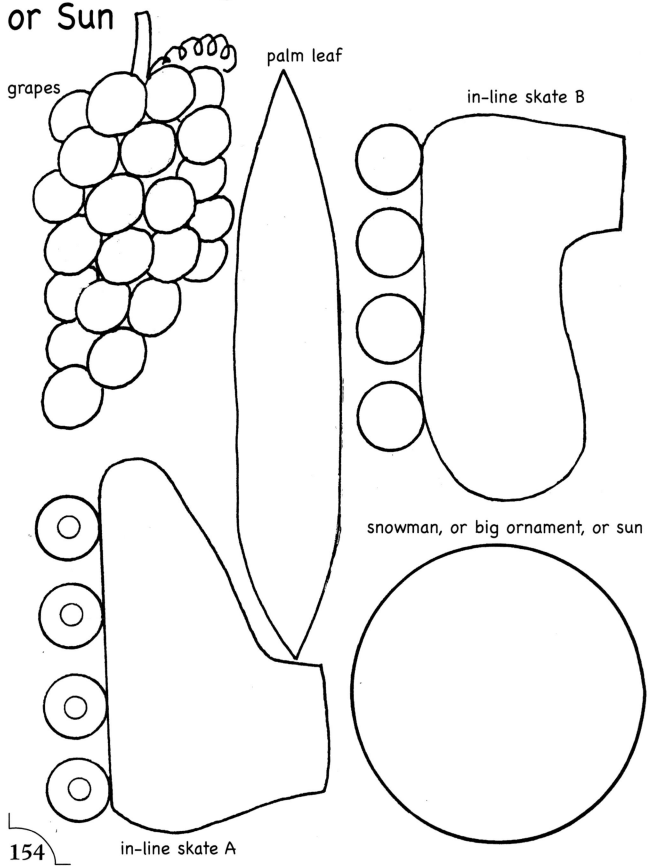

grapes

palm leaf

in-line skate B

snowman, or big ornament, or sun

in-line skate A

hamster

Hearts,
Turtles,
Fish,
Hamster

little fish

baby turtle

big turtle

big/little hearts
medium heart

Heart, Bird, Tree Trunk, Trees A and B

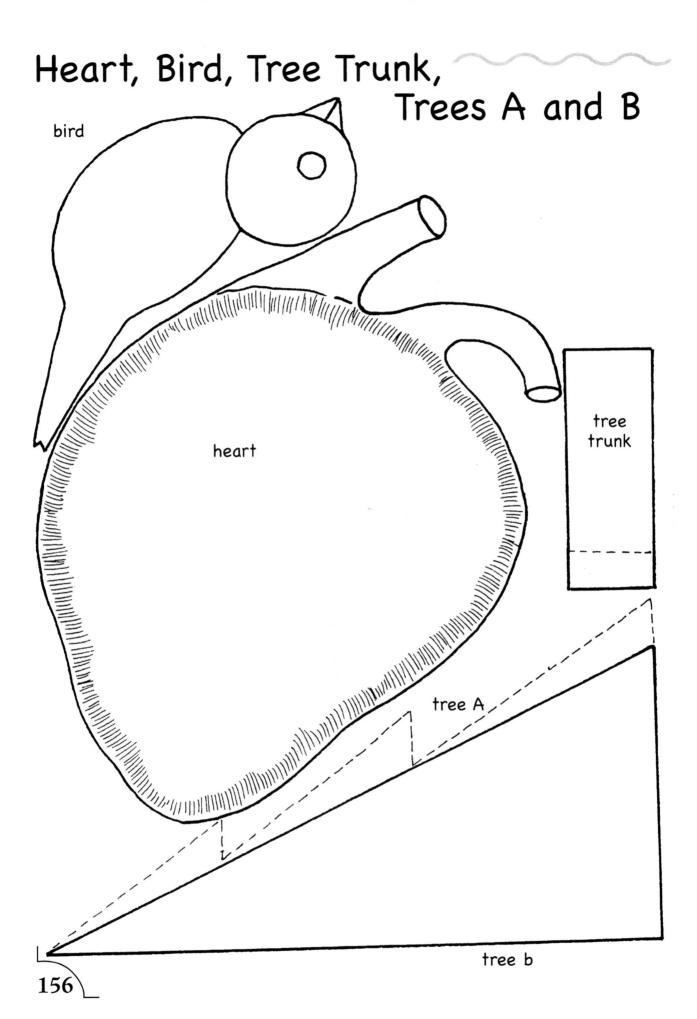

bird

heart

tree trunk

tree A

tree b

Seat Belt, Water, Boys, Water Drops

boy
(water)

boy
(light switch)

water drops

seat belt

BUCKLE UP!

Peppers, Vine, Dog, Chestnut, Flowers A and B

dog

chestnut

flower A

vine

flower B

peppers

Pumpkin,
Steps,
Black Walnut,
Walnut, Car

steps

pumpkin

walnut

black walnut

car

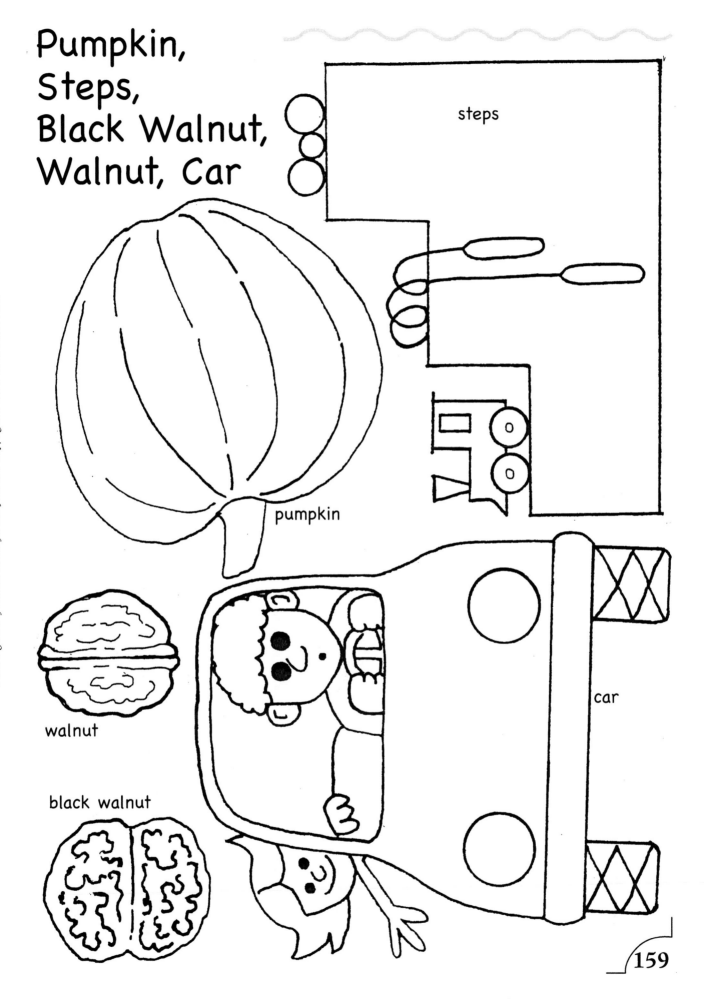

George Washington, Squirrel

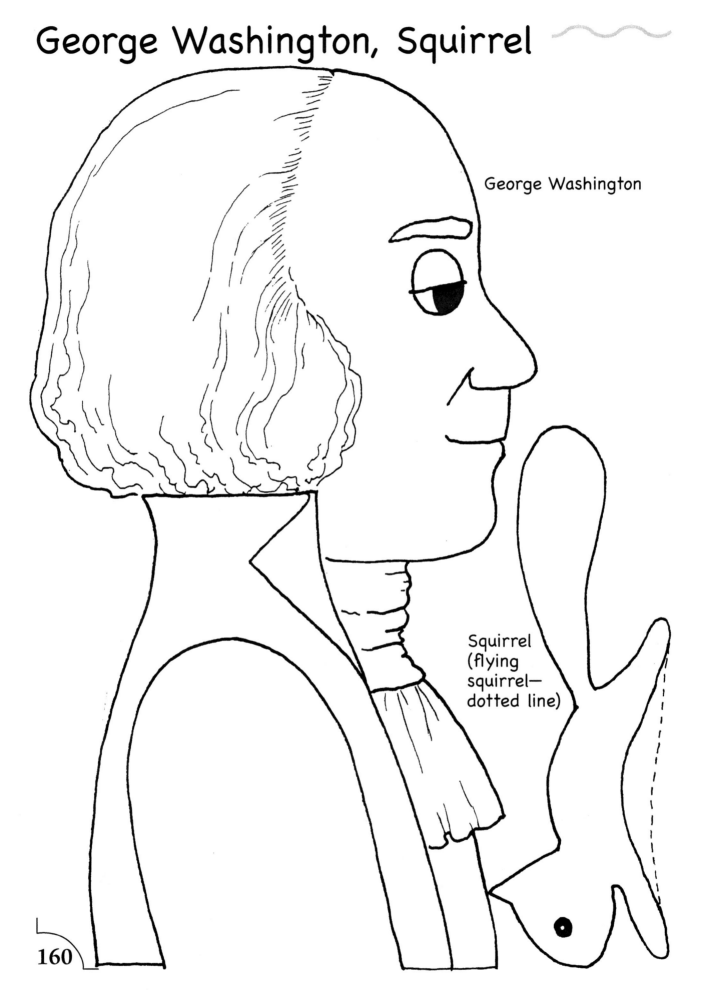

George Washington

Squirrel
(flying
squirrel—
dotted line)

Washington's Arm, Lettuce, Root, Umbrella, Handle

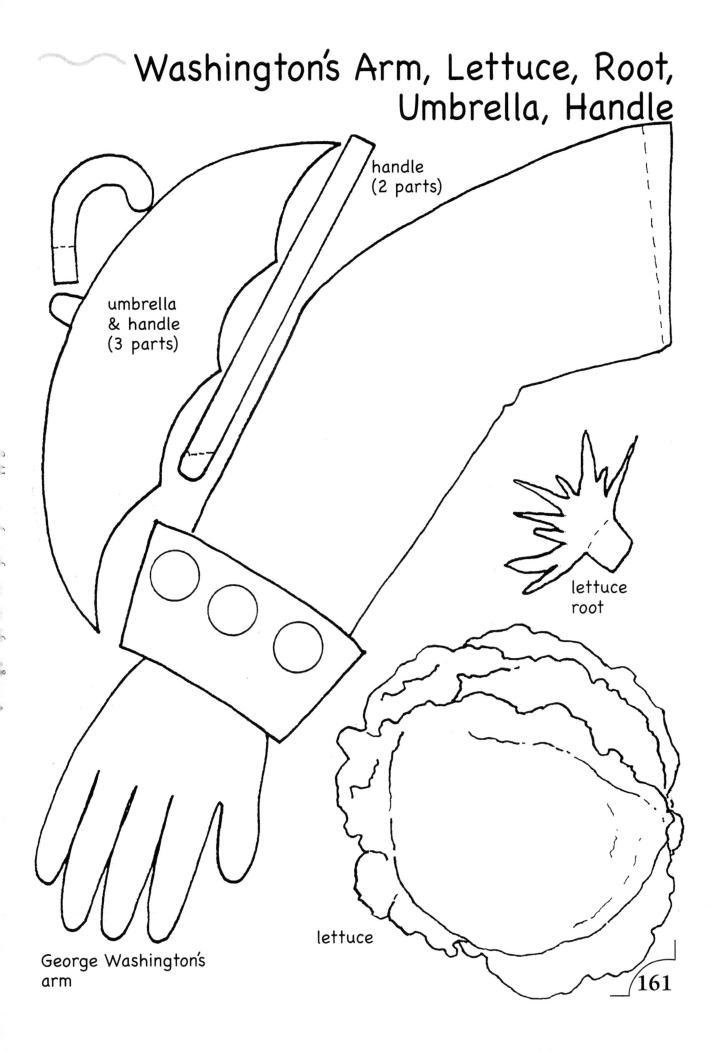

handle
(2 parts)

umbrella
& handle
(3 parts)

lettuce
root

lettuce

George Washington's
arm

161

Palm Leaves, Butterfly, Frog, Toucan, Christmas Cactus, Snake Plant

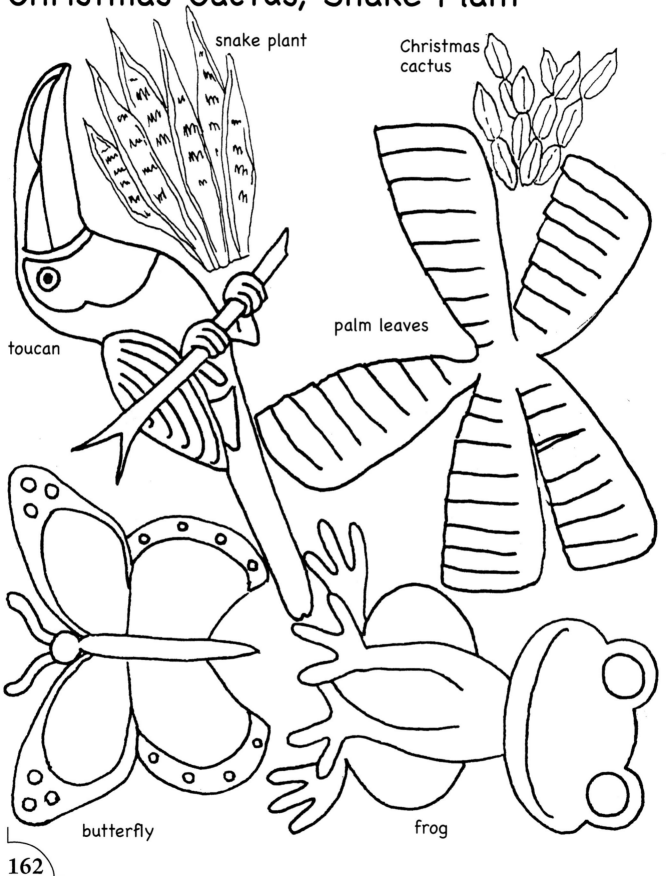

snake plant

Christmas cactus

toucan

palm leaves

butterfly

frog

House, Smoke, Bird

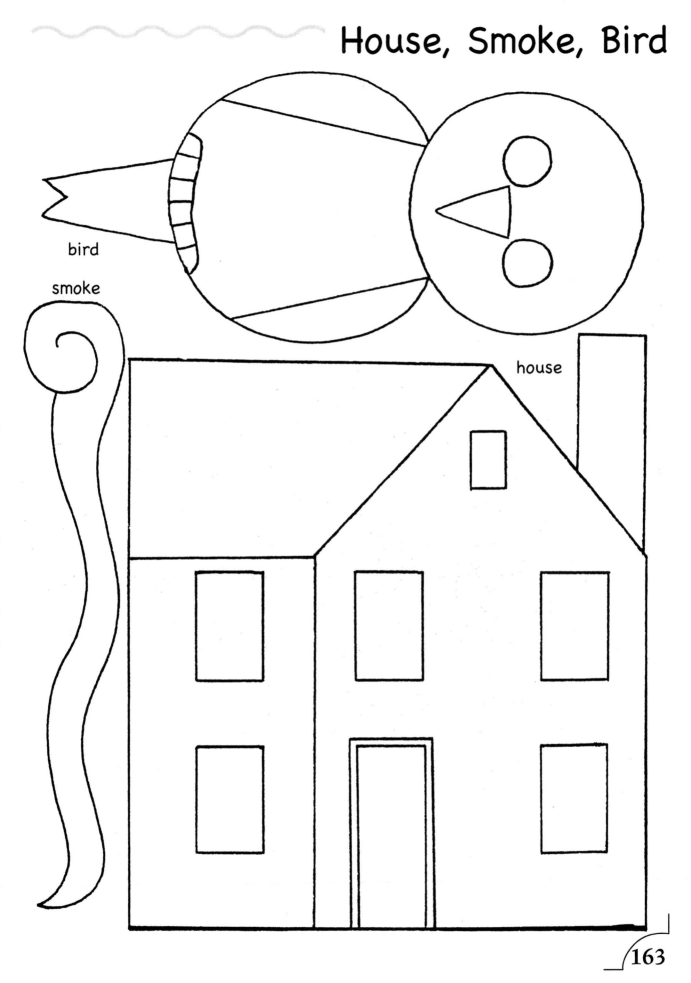

bird

smoke

house

Face, Kite, Shamrock

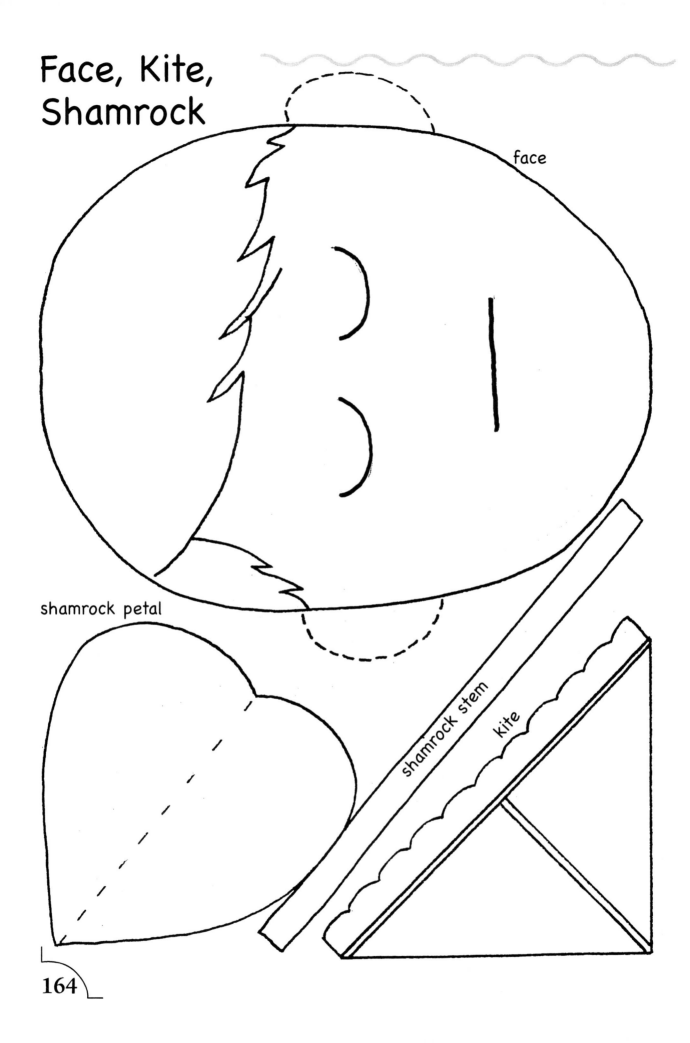

face

shamrock petal

shamrock stem

kite

Cow, Pig, Cat, Chicken

pig

cow

cat

chicken

165

Horse, Sheep

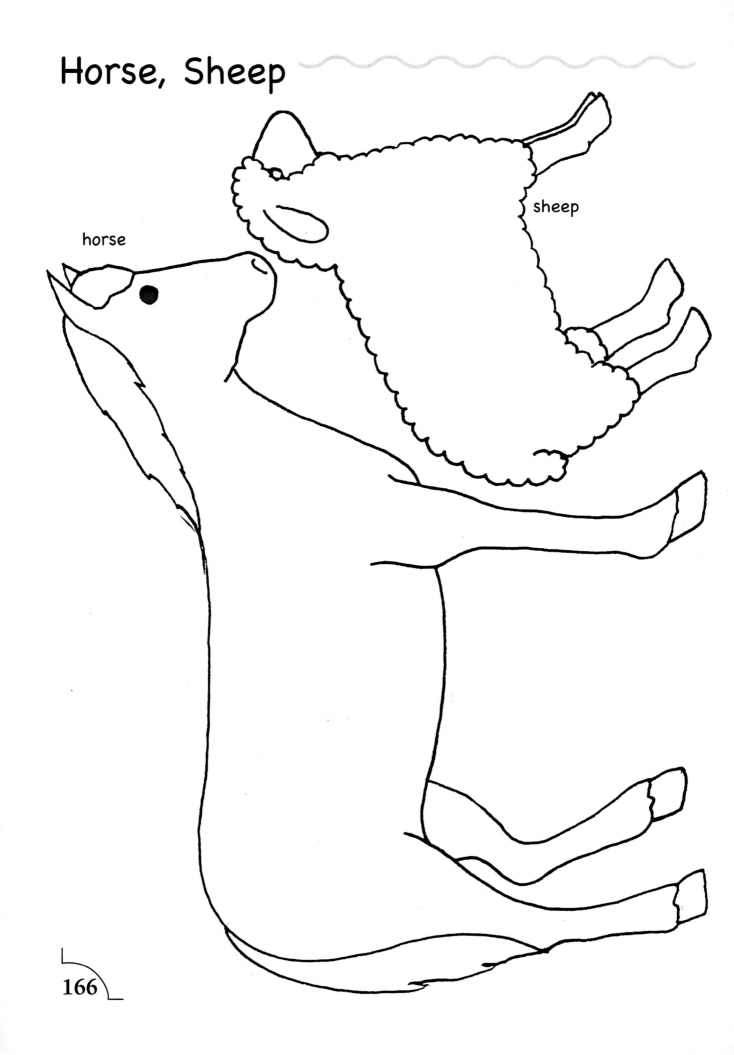

horse

sheep

Red Cross Helmet, Hen

Red Cross helmet

hen

Flower, Root, Milk, Cheese, Ice Cream, Yogurt, Butter

flower

root

ice cream

ICE CREAM

yogurt

YOGURT

BUTTER

butter

cheese

milk

grass

truck

MILK
TANK TRUCK

dairy

DAIRY

Face, Hand, Raincoat, Arm, Angry Mouth

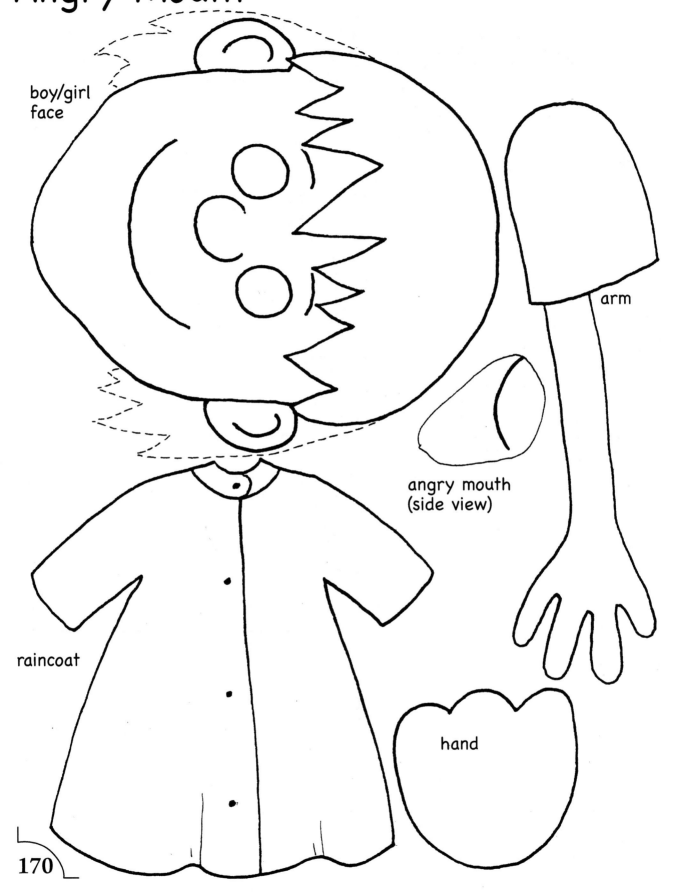

boy/girl
face

arm

angry mouth
(side view)

raincoat

hand

flames

logs

Bears, Flower, Cloud, Puppy

bear
and cub

big
flower

cloud/puppy

Dog, Cat

cat

dog

173

Egg, Nest, Book, Matzos

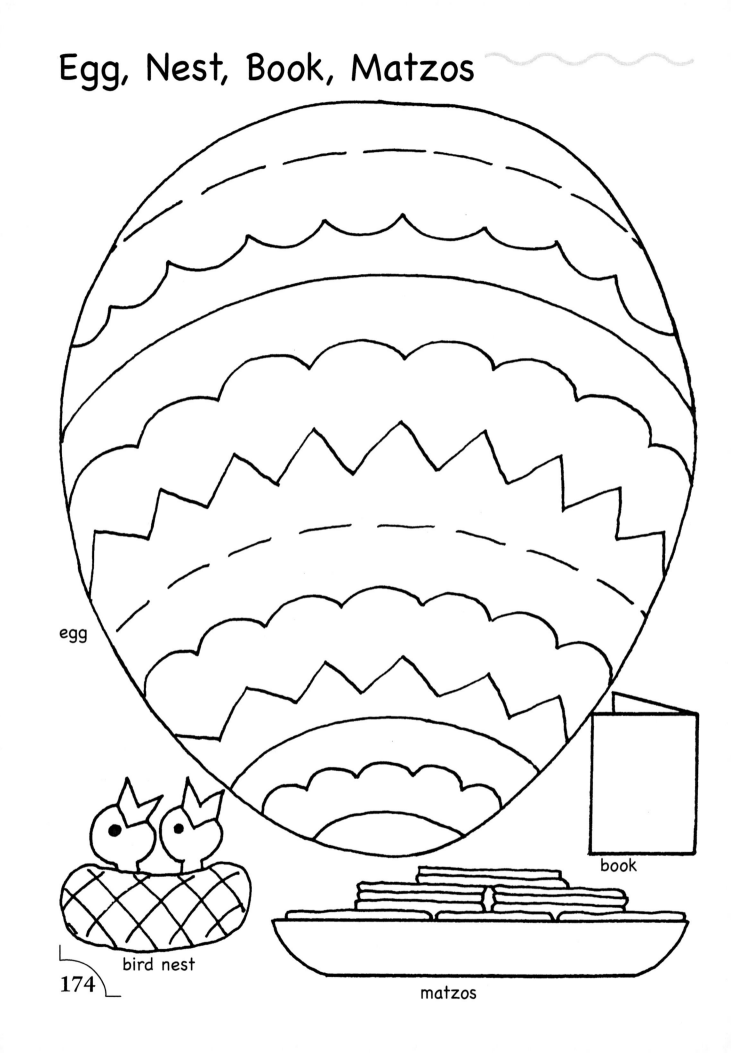

egg

bird nest

book

matzos

Green Bean Plant, Insect, Chipmunk

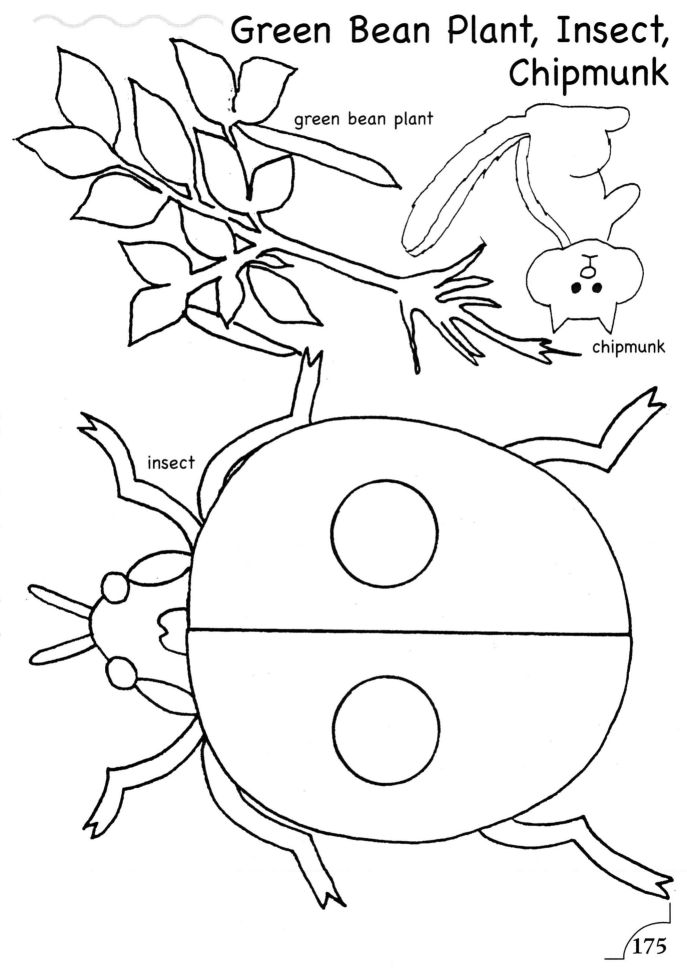

green bean plant

chipmunk

insect

Cow, Corn, Snake, Snowballs

snowballs

snake

cow

corn

Flower, Pig, Picnic Jug, Sun

stem—cut 1
leaves—cut 2

big flower

pig

sun

picnic jug

177

Barn

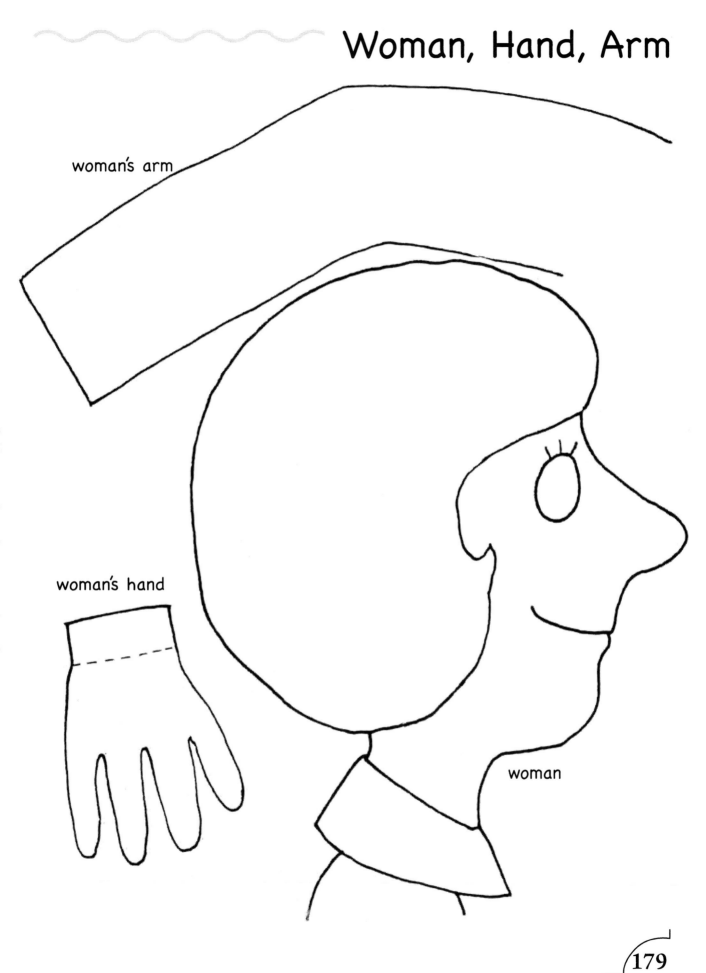

Woman, Hand, Arm

woman's arm

woman's hand

woman

179

Uncle Sam

From Big Book of Bulletin Boards for Every Month Copyright © 2006 Good Year Books

Hat, Flag, Instruments, Tomato

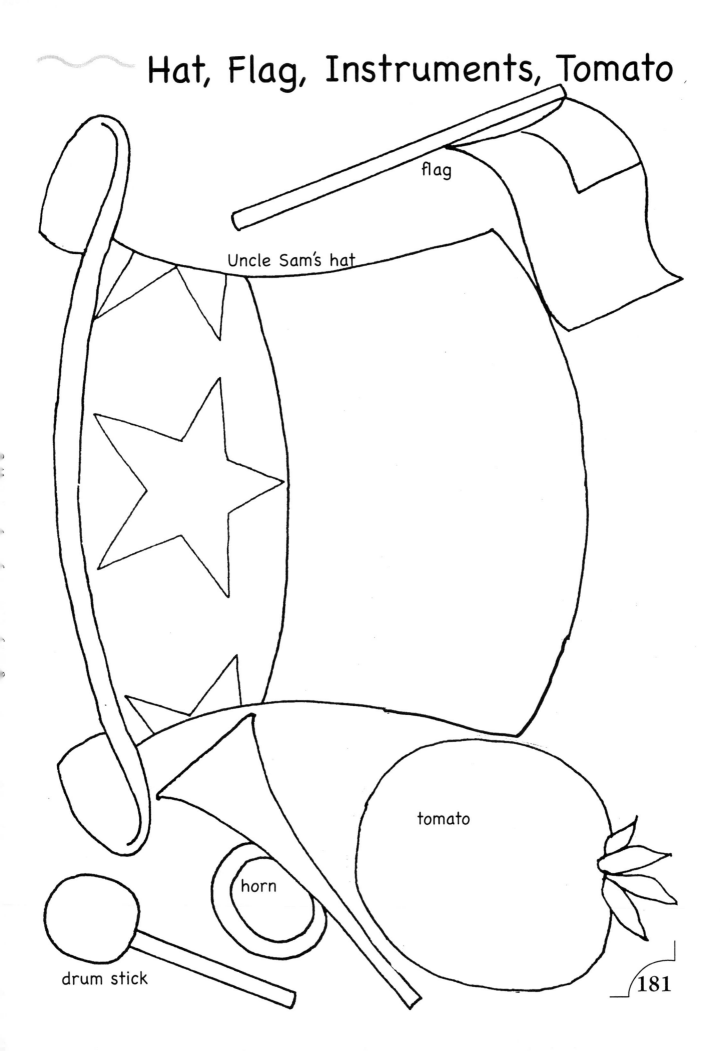

flag

Uncle Sam's hat

tomato

horn

drum stick

Flag, Hand, Cookie A and B

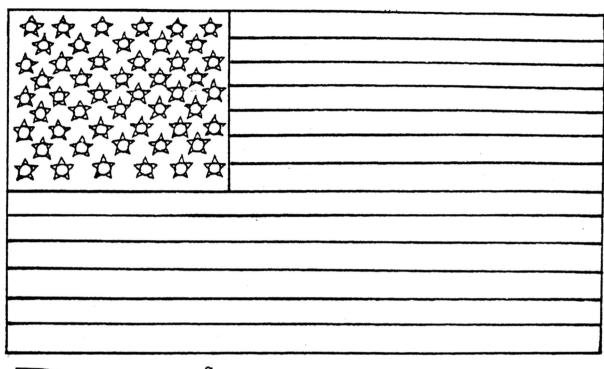

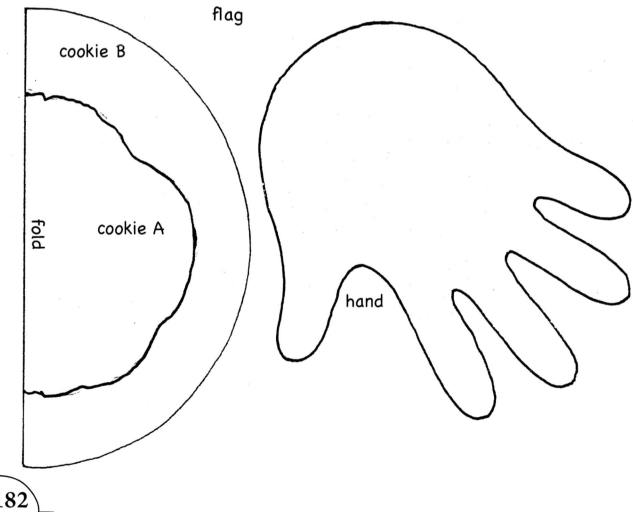

flag

cookie B

fold

cookie A

hand

Fireworks

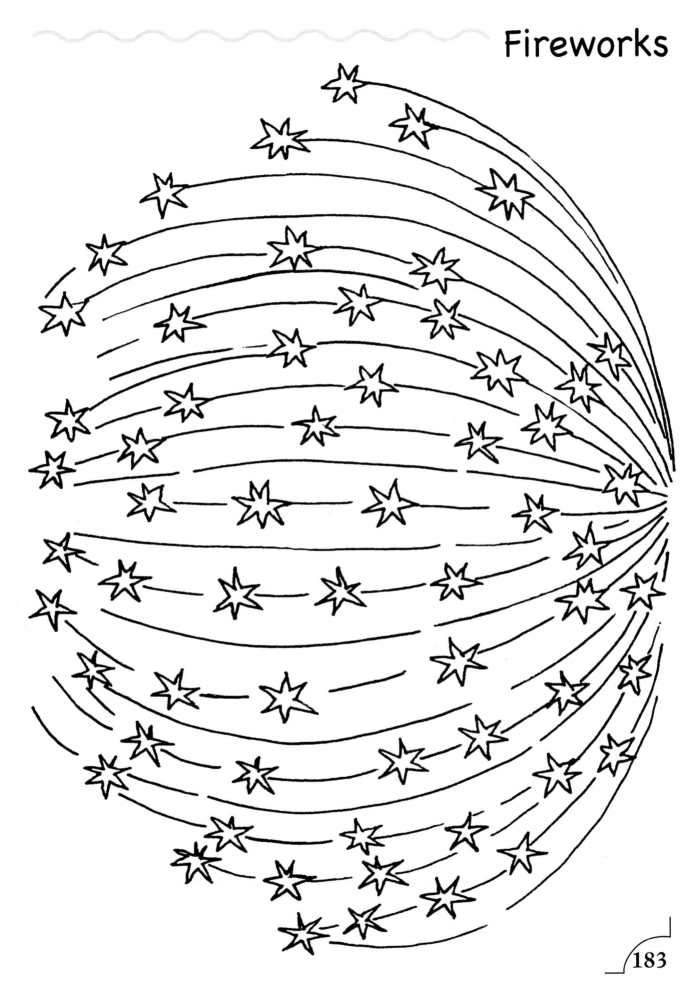

Fish, Sailboat, Sandwiches, Pancakes, Dreidel

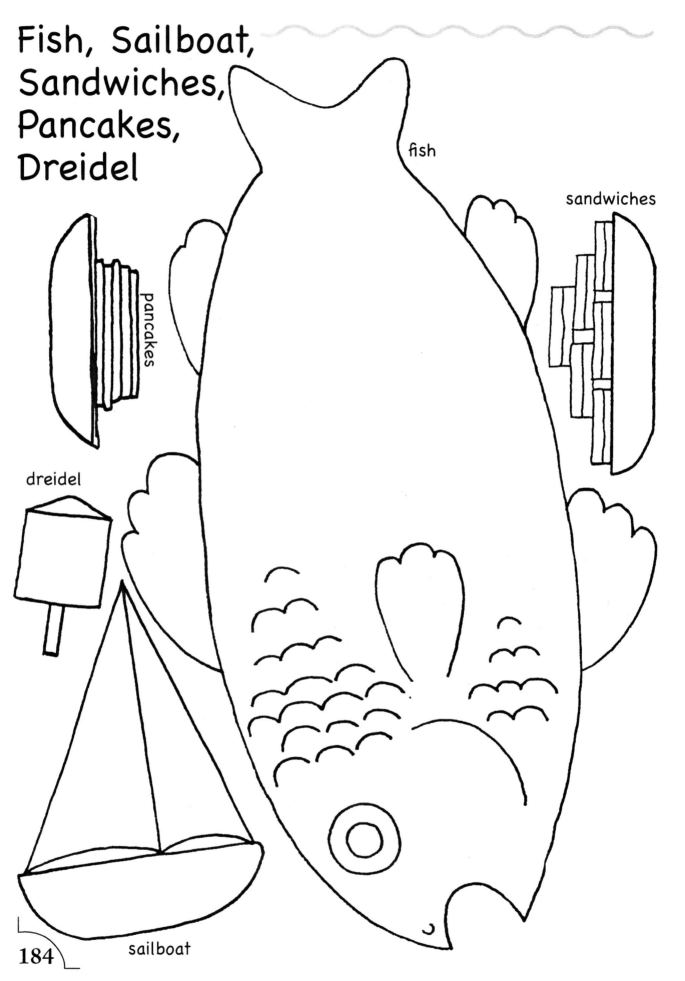

fish

sandwiches

pancakes

dreidel

sailboat

Ferris Wheel, Tomato Plant

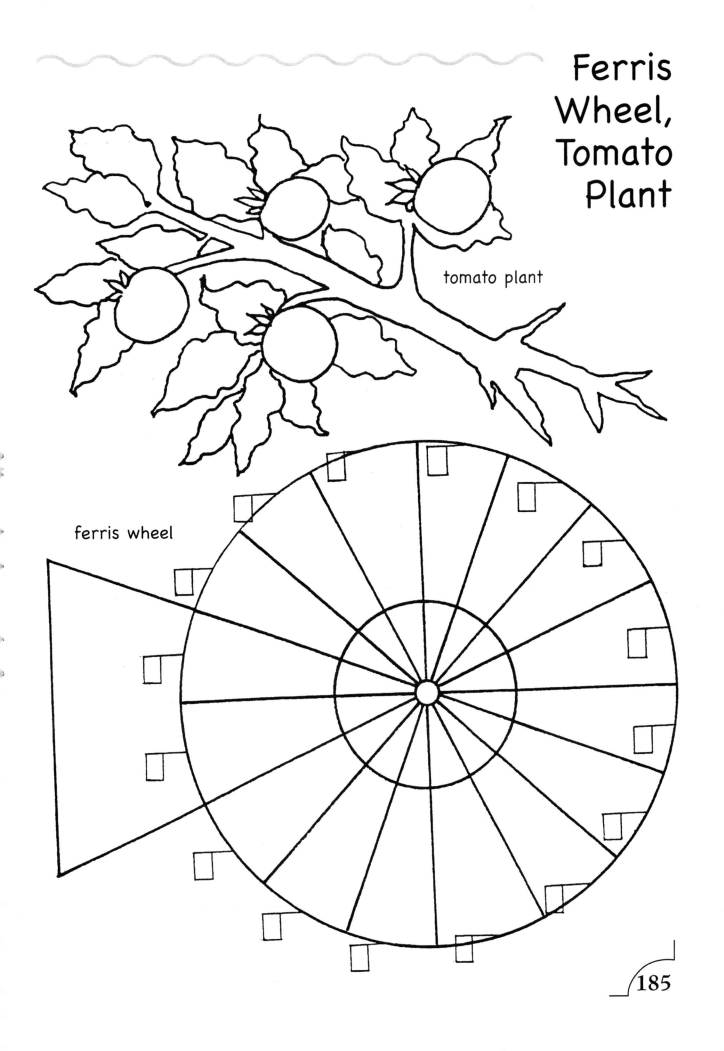

tomato plant

ferris wheel

185

My Bulletin Board Ideas

My Bulletin Board Ideas

My Bulletin Board Ideas

My Bulletin Board Ideas

My Bulletin Board Ideas

My Bulletin Board Ideas

My Bulletin Board Ideas